BARRENNESS:
Journey to God's Divine Provision

BLANCHE CLIPPER HUDSON

WESTBOW°
PRESS
A DIVISION OF THOMAS NELSON
& ZONDERVAN

WestBow Press books may be ordered through booksellers or by contacting:

WestBow Press
A Division of Thomas Nelson & Zondervan
1663 Liberty Drive
Bloomington, IN 47403
www.westbowpress.com
1 (866) 928-1240

ISBN: 978-1-4908-8952-8 (sc)
ISBN: 978-1-4908-8954-2 (hc)
ISBN: 978-1-4908-8953-5 (e)

Library of Congress Control Number: 2015916646

Print information available on the last page.

WestBow Press rev. date: 08/07/2015

Note:

In this manuscript the references to Abram and Sarai refer to their
"pre-covenant names" in Scripture before God changed their names
to Abraham and Sarah (Genesis 17:5-19). When God established His
covenant with Abram, He changed their names to Abraham and
Sarah to signify His covenant agreement with them as the father of
many nations (Genesis 17:5) and mother of nations (Genesis 17:16).

Contents

Dedicated to
The memory of
Women who nurtured me –
Blanche Warren Clipper (paternal grandmother)
Viola Whitby Clipper (mother)
Annie Whitby Wood (maternal great-grandmother)
Lula Whitby Sullivan and
Viola Whitby Shamwell (maternal great-aunts)

Foreword

"Barrenness can be God's own method of divine provisioning..." is an excerpt from a powerful declaration that Blanche Hudson makes in her book *Barrenness: Journey to God's Divine Provision*. Hudson uses this statement as one method to draw the reader into taking a thought provoking and engaging journey with her to learn how barrenness was a degrading and social stigma for married women in ancient biblical times. Yet, in God's infinite wisdom and providential planning, barrenness and birth are significant and inclusive of the movement of God in our lives. Although barrenness is viewed by many then and even today as a disgrace or socially uncomfortable, God loves and works in and through the lives of women and men who are barren. In fact, Hudson points out through real life stories and her personal testimonies that barrenness opens up many opportunities for new life in ways that are surprising, delightful, and hopeful.

Through the biblical worldview, we are guided through Hudson's work to experience how God created blessings of new lives that were revealed when life circumstances dictated something differently. As Hudson notes, "Tikva Frymer-Kensky points out that, 'The infertility of the matriarchs has two effects: (1) it heightens the drama of the birth of the eventual son, marking Isaac, Jacob and Joseph as special; and (2) it emphasizes that pregnancy is an act of God'. Therefore, barrenness for a period of time shows that new life is a divine intervention."

In the world of the five women, Sarai, Hannah, Rebekah, Rachel, and Manoah's wife, (one of the many unnamed women in the Bible), introduced or re-introduced to us by Hudson, we see how their marriage to wealthy and powerful men in the land or the love of their husband, cannot make them happy or complete. The women's desire to have a child is greater than anything their husband can promise or give to them. Their empty wombs are heavy burdens to the women, but surprisingly, we do not hear the husbands complaining to the women about not having a child. Although Jacob does respond to Rachel's demand for a child by declaring that she should take her desire for a child to God and not to burden him with such a request (Genesis 30:1-2).

Hudson's passion for God's compassion and fulfillment in the lives of women who are barren (and in our everyday lives), writes in descriptive ways how God intentionally cares about the emptiness and heartache that these women have experienced. Uplifting God's Words through the prophet Isaiah and in Psalms, Hudson shares with us God's care for women who are barren. The Prophet Isaiah says, "*Sing, O barren one who did not bear; burst into song and shout, …For the LORD has called you like a wife forsaken and grieved in spirit"* (Isaiah 54:1, 6). The Psalmist voice rings out the message of faith: "*He gives the barren woman a home, making her the joyous mother of children. Praise the Lord"* (Psalm 113:9).

It is insightful to read the connection that Hudson makes between the planting, growing, new life, and barrenness. This agricultural society depended upon the land for their food from their crops, the animals to graze, and for the land to produce their livelihood in many ways. Having land that was their own, fertile, and was God's gift to God's people, was a blessing. Yet, God's chosen people, would often turn their back on God, and then their lives would be barren in many ways. Therefore, having children strengthened the family's ability to support itself in the present and future.

Children represented legacy and possible financial strength. Not having a child, a male child in particular, was looked upon as a disgrace.

God's divine provision in barrenness is revealed through the miracle in the births and the lives of Isaac to Sarai, 90 years old, and Abraham, 100 years old; Samuel to Hannah, who looked drunk, but prayed fervently and faithfully for a child for many years; Joseph and Benjamin born to Rachel, who was the love of Jacob's life; and Samson to a nameless mother, who is simply known as Manoah's wife. Although they were socially ridiculed, God had a greater plan for their lives, and the world. As Hudson declares "God's divine purpose in barrenness is to bring glory to Him." God's ways our truly not our ways!

Hudson carefully reminds us in *Barrenness: Journey to God's Divine Provision* that we need to expand our understanding of barrenness and its practical application in our spiritual, theological, social, and psychological experiences. As we participate with Hudson in this journey from barrenness toward a stronger relationship with God, our barren moments or long-term empty places in our lives become more evident. Barrenness in some ways may be permanent, but it is a place of promise and possibilities that we can grow from and give to others and ourselves. It is painful and discouraging at times, but Hudson reminds us that trusting God and not allowing barrenness to be our god, yields new life in ways that only God can give to us.

Cheryl Price, Ph. D.
Author and co-author of several
books for Urban Ministries, Inc.
Editor-at-Large, Urban Ministries, Inc.

Acknowledgments

To my pastor, Dr. H. Beecher Hicks, Jr. who gave suggestions about revisions and publication while writing the book; I am deeply grateful for his wisdom, knowledge and advice.

To Dr. Cheryl Price, a special friend and the first person who encouraged me to pursue publication; she provided support throughout the whole journey. I am deeply grateful for her friendship and support.

To Dr. Beverly Mitchell, professor, Wesley Theological Seminary, who read and critiqued the manuscript and made several helpful suggestions on the content. I offer sincere gratitude for her very generous comments.

To Dr. Jocelyn Johnson, a fellow clergy who gave inspirational help; I am deeply thankful for her insightful, teaching spirit.

To Rev. Dr. Samuel Lynch, a fellow clergy and friend who introduced me to two special people that became immensely helpful as a resource while writing this book. Many thanks.

To Mrs. Shirley Jackson and Ms. Dominique Evans, members of Metropolitan Baptist Church PUSH Ministry who prayed for me and offered much encouragement; I thank you.

To Ms. Shunita Seacrease, a friend who provided helpful suggestions and encouragement; I offer my deep appreciation.

To Mrs. Joanna Politano, a fellow writer, who critiqued the manuscript in its early stages and offered insightful suggestions. I am deeply grateful for her kind and generous assistance.

To Mrs. Patricia Adkins, a friend who edited the manuscript and provided guidance in completion of the book, I offer sincere gratitude.

Excerpt from Howard Thurman's Pen regarding Man's Journey

Man's (woman's) journey is hazardous because the world in which he (she) lives is grounded in order and held intact by an inner and irresistible logic, by laws that, in one vast creative sweep encompass the infinite variety of the universe and give life its stability, but at the same time make living anywhere, at any time, a dramatic risk for any particular unit of life, be it man (woman) or plant. It is on such a stage, in such a setting, that the drama of the private life and the collective enterprises of man (woman) are played. Though suffering is a private encounter, and in the last analysis a man (woman) must deal with it in solitariness and isolation, it is ultimately reassuring if it can be placed in a frame of reference as universal and comprehensive as life itself.[1]

---

1   Howard Thurman, *A Strange Freedom*, Beacon Press: Boston, Mass, 1998, 37.

CHAPTER ONE

The Prologue

◇◇◇◇◇

I would like to introduce you to five Hebrew matriarchs who experienced decades of distress in their marriage because they were barren for many years. These are no ordinary women - they each have extraordinary characteristics. In fact, two of the matriarchs, Hannah and Manoah's wife, showed great faith in God's power to deliver them from the shame and disgrace of barrenness; they demonstrated confidence and hope for what they could not see, standing as exemplars of great faith. This book is about each of the five matriarchs' miraculous conception and birth of a son after decades of barrenness, even after menopause in Sarai's case. What is even more interesting is that the sons born through the miraculous birth was God's own provision for Israel's leadership during critical times in her history.

Barrenness can be God's own method of divine provisioning for His people through the phenomena of barren women. Even when the patriarchs made unwise and selfish decisions that placed their wives in compromising situations, and God's plans and purposes seem to be in jeopardy, they are never thwarted through the actions of humankind. On the contrary, God's plans are manifested through the miracle and mystery of grace.

Never ridiculed by their husbands for being barren, these beloved wives were marginalized and considered a disgrace in the community due to the agrarian society in which they lived that depended on the land for survival, male labor for keeping flock, and planting and harvesting crops. Emotionally, the wives deepest distress was assuming responsibility for their barren condition; they internalized the misery of not fulfilling their maternal role of birthing sons. Except for Isaac who prayed for his wife to conceive, it was the matriarchs who tried to provide a solution to the barrenness problem. There was another reason for women in Abram's family to feel distress for not birthing a son. God had made a covenant with Abram to multiply his seed. And with each generation, the wives are barren for many years.

This book is about the phenomena of the five Hebrew matriarchs' journey from barrenness to fruitfulness through God's divine intervention; three from Abram's family and Hannah and Manoah's wife are the other two. These five wives were barren, but later gave birth to sons who became Israel's leaders. Sarai and Rachel tried to solve the problem by giving their handmaids to their husbands to produce a child through surrogacy.

Surrogacy was an accepted practice of ancient Near East culture as an alternative of producing an heir. According to *The Hammurabi Codes*, sections 145 and 146, "Surrogacy provided a way to have an heir who could retain land and property holdings in the family" (*The Ancient Near East*, 1958). But surrogacy often had its negative effects; for example, rivalry between the biological and surrogate mothers, recall what occurred between Sarai and Hagar. Instead of waiting on God, Sarai became impatient. But God was specific with Abram after he had fathered Ishmael with Hagar. God specifically told Abram in His promise that his heir would come from Sarai's own body. However, it was several years later after Ishmael was born that God opened Sarai's womb - she conceived the Promised Child, Isaac. Then Sarai instructed her husband to send Hagar and her son away because she did not want him to inherit along with her own son, Isaac, the baby she conceived and birthed after menopause.

Chapter one gives an overall introduction to the book about the theme and the five Hebrew women. It also mentions that there are problems the matriarchs face due to the patriarchs' unwise decisions.

Chapter two describes the barrenness phenomenon as a divine act of God and lists examples of barren women who later conceived as well as examples of barren women who remained childless. The chapter also addresses the function and purpose of the study, the scope and rationale. Cultural aspects and laws regarding surrogacy in ancient Israel illumine the reasons some barren women opted to use this method as a means of covering their shame.

While reviewing the literature for chapter three, important areas emerged that will be discussed more fully in later chapters; namely, (1) the women's active protest of their barrenness (Havrelock, 2008), (2) how this affected the relationship with their husbands and (3) their relationship with God (Callaway, 1986; Baskin, 1989).

Chapter four provides personal stories from barren women of the Bible, one couple's awesome testimony about using one of the Assisted Reproductive Technology methods, and another woman's report of how she prayed and asked God for a child when she was told by the doctors that she could not have children - God intervened and gave new life to all of these barren women.

Chapter five discusses some patriarchal problems that present another dimension to this study in terms of their actions and decision that seemingly place Abram's seed in jeopardy. Both Abram and Isaac made decisions to save their own lives, thus affecting their wives' safety whenever they encountered kings on their journey. Two patriarchs, in particular, demonstrated a lack of faith in God to protect them.

In chapter six, I share a sermon that addresses relevant principles of God's fruitfulness from the scripture Isaiah 54 that highlights the theological aspect of the barren wife motif. In addition, I use illustrations from my own personal experience during a season of feeling spiritually barren. Moreover, God showed me some things about my own ministry and I could see a relationship between the physically barren women's pain and my own feelings of distress. Therefore, chapter six is also my testimony and what I learned about the principles of fruitfulness.

Chapter seven discloses the sociological aspect for women and men who are physically barren. This chapter provides information for those who may desire to know more about the use of various Assisted Reproductive Technology (ART) methods as an alternative to infertility. Subjects that might be considered "Frequently Asked Questions" about the ethics behind Christian couples (1) pursuing ART as an alternative to infertility, (2) the alternatives to a natural conception and (3) whether or not they should use some form of ART. This material will assist infertile couples to have conversations with their spiritual advisor and medical practitioner about these subjects. However, the information in the help section is meant to be a resource guide to aid couples in making informed decisions, along with their pastor and medical practitioner.

Chapter eight summarizes the barren women's voices in praises to God for deliverance from barrenness as an expression of the wisdom gained through the barrenness years. Each matriarch conceived, and gave birth to a male child, a son who would rise up to be one of Israel's leaders - none of the mothers knew God's ultimate plan and purpose for her son. Without the knowledge of God's plans - Hannah, a woman of strong faith - dedicated her son to the Lord before he was conceived. When he was born she sang a hymn of praise to the Giver of new life.

In conclusion, the ***Journey Study Guide*** provides an ideal teaching tool for small groups to continue and extend the learning experience about the phenomena of barrenness. The format provides an interesting guide for focus groups, Christian counselors or pastors to use as a resource for study or discussion. The ***Journey Study Guide*** is also adaptable for individual study.

NOTES

CHAPTER TWO

The Pathway To The Journey

◇◇◇◇◇

The subject of barrenness has long intrigued me since I first discovered the number of women in Scripture who had been barren and then gave birth, especially the women in Abraham's family. What intrigued me most, why would God promise to multiply Abraham's seed and then make all the women barren? With each succeeding generation, Abraham's seed was in danger of dying out because the wives remained childless. This heightened the expectation for a baby for many years. The first matriarch Sarai was ninety years old when Isaac was born. In the second generation, Isaac's wife, Rebekah was barren for twenty years before Isaac prayed for God to open her womb. In the third generation, Rachel and Leah were married to Jacob and both were barren for some years. Then God opened Leah's womb when He saw that she was hated, but the one Jacob really loved, Rachel, remained barren for many more years. Then God remembered Rachel and opened her womb.[1] Can you imagine the shame these wives must have endured for not producing an heir after years of marriage? Can you feel Rachel's longing for a baby when

---

1   Scriptures say God remembered the barren women, Genesis 30:22 and I Samuel 1:19. God also remembered the house of Israel, Psalm 98:3 and God remembered us, Psalm 136:23 and Isaiah 49:14.

she cried to Jacob, "Give me children or else I die?" Barren women carried within their bosom a feeling of emptiness and heartache known as twin sorrows.

Although barrenness is a most intriguing subject, the astounding fact that it occurred three times in Abraham's family, the man whose seed God promised to bless with numerous offspring, is phenomenal. Each generation from Abram to Jacob, the matriarch was barren. How amazing was that! Also, another interesting incidence is that while Abram and Sarai journeyed from place to place, the barrenness phenomena affected others whom they encountered on their journey. Because Abram was afraid the king would kill him and take Sarai for a wife, he lied about his relationship to Sarai saying, "She is my sister." So God even closed the maidservants' wombs in the king's house - they were cursed because Sarai was taken into his household. Abram's deception seemingly placed his seed in jeopardy; but God promised him that his heir would be birthed through Sarai. Twice, God intervened and rescued Sarai to preserve and restore her to Abram as his wife.

The Phenomenon of Barrenness

Barrenness is an unusual and inexplicable mystery. However, God is able to intervene in our barren condition, but we must be willing to participate in our own deliverance. Although barrenness is a physical condition, it can be a spiritual existence as well and the desire to be fruitful is a longing felt by heartache, too. Why do some women, even when trying to conceive, remain childless after many years of marriage? The Hebrew word for barren is *agar* which means a woman who is childless. Scholars say, "In the East, barrenness was considered a reproach and punishment from God. The reproach attached to barrenness especially among the Hebrews was due to the expectation of the Messiah and the hope cherished by every woman that she might be the mother of the Promised Seed."[2]

Other Hebrew Wives Who Were Barren

The phenomenon of barrenness was not limited to Abram's family. Scripture records other Hebrew matriarchs who were barren. During the period of the judges, an unnamed matriarch, referred to only as Manoah's wife, remained childless for several years. She is one of the many unnamed women in the Bible. Manoah's wife was visited by an angel who told her that she would conceive, but Manoah doubted and questioned the angel's pronouncement. Manoah's wife was a woman of faith and believed God; she had confidence in what the angel told her.

Hannah, the mother of the prophet Samuel, was another great woman of faith. She also had no children for many years before giving birth to her first child. Unlike Sarai, Hannah had a trusting response to her childless condition and she demonstrated her faith with works: (1) she went to the temple; (2) fervently prayed and petitioned God for a man-child; (3) vowed to dedicate him to God before the baby was conceived in her womb; and (4) gave the gift back to the Giver as her act of faith. Hannah's prayer is a model for all Christians seeking an answer from God by participating in her deliverance. After Hannah made her petition, she fulfilled her vow by an act of faith, and lends her son to the Lord for as long as he lived.

Prayer Overheard by the Temple Priest

Hannah's demonstrative prayer attracted the temple priest, Eli, who saw her lips moving while she was praying in the

---

2　*The New Unger's Bible Dictionary*, Merrill F. Unger, Database 2003 Wordsearch Corp., Moody Press: Chicago, Ill., 1988.

temple. Eli assumed she had been drinking and questioned her demeanor, but Hannah defended her actions. Then Eli pronounced God's blessing on Hannah's prayer, although she did not tell him what she had prayed for. When she and her husband returned from the temple, Hannah was intimate with him and this time God intervened. Consequently, when she and Elkanah had sexual relations, this time Hannah conceived.

Is there a Relationship between Physical and Spiritual Barrenness?

Although I had served five years as an interim minister, when I applied to several churches and received rejection letters and closed doors, I felt barren because I desired to be in a pastoral position. Rejection is what I experienced after not receiving a "call" to a pastoral position. During that time of waiting, I began to question whether God had another place for me to serve. Then God moved unexpectedly and opened up another door.

God is ever-new in His ways of answering our prayers. The answer came through an unusual invitation to a luncheon meeting with a friend who had invited others I had not expected. The reason I say unusual is because I usually invite my out-of-town friend to have lunch at my home whenever she is in town. This time, she invited me to join her and others to have lunch at a restaurant. I was happy to join them. At the restaurant, seated between a father and his son, I was asked by the father (who was a pastor) if I would consider coming to serve as his Minister for Christian Education because his current minister had accepted another position. The invitation surprised me for two reasons: first, I had served with him in my first ministerial position as Minister for Children and Youth and; second, I was totally unprepared to respond. That luncheon meeting was a turning point in my ministry.

I learned two lessons from that experience: (1) be willing to receive a gift from a friend as well as to give a gift of hospitality, and (2) you can be blessed in unexpected ways by opening your heart with gratitude to what others want to give to you. After praying for God's direction, I accepted the minister's invitation. The next year, the pastor asked me to be his executive pastor; this time I immediately accepted because God had spoken to me about stepping up to more pastoral responsibility. God had provided the opportunity of serving again in a pastoral role.

The Function of Barrenness

Tikva Frymer-Kensky points out that, "The infertility of the matriarchs has two effects: (1) it heightens the drama of the birth of the eventual son, marking Isaac, Jacob and Joseph as special; and (2) it emphasizes that pregnancy is an act of God". Therefore, barrenness for a period of time shows that new life is a divine intervention. When a barren woman gives birth, it is not by way of generation, but the work of divine power. This is especially noted in the example of Sarai, who was ninety years old when she conceived Isaac (Genesis 21:1-2). Scripture also show another example; Elizabeth in the New Testament (Luke 1:7, 13) was postmenstrual when she conceived John after many years of barrenness.

Does A Woman's Menopausal Age and Years of Infertility Affect her Ability to be Fruitful?

Although post- menopausal, a barren woman's body will function in accordance with God's will and purpose when He intervenes. Therefore, barrenness functions both as a passive and a receptive object for divine initiative and grace. After Isaac prayed for God to open Rebekah's womb, she conceived twins, although she had been infertile for 20 years (Genesis 25:21-22). Following years of childlessness and rivalry with her sister, God remembered Rachel and opened her womb, although she had been barren. Rachel conceived and bore a son and named him Joseph (Genesis 30:22). Before the miraculous births occurred, these matriarchs had such a strong desire to have a baby; their sorrow and grief was so overwhelming they gave their handmaids to their husbands to have a baby for them. Barrenness was a mark of disgrace in Israel's culture; but it was also a sign that God was the cause of their barren condition. One can only imagine the great anticipation and joy these women experienced when they felt that first flutter of life.

God's Divine Purpose of Barrenness

God's divine purpose in barrenness is to bring glory to Him. In his book, *Lectures on Systematic Theology*, Charles Finney discusses ten topics on "the purposes of God" that are relevant and pertinent to our study. Finney's ten topics are:

1. What I understand by the purposes of God.
2. Distinction between purposes and decree.
3. There must be some sense in which God's purposes extend to all events.
4. Different sense in which God purposes different events.
5. God's revealed will is never inconsistent with His secret purpose.
6. Wisdom and benevolence of the purposes of God.
7. The immutability of the divine purposes.
8. The purposes of God are a ground of eternal and joyful confidence.
9. The relation of God's purposes to His prescience or foreknowledge.

10. God's purposes are not inconsistent, but demand the use of means both on His part, and on our part, to accomplish them.

God continues to demonstrate that He is the Giver of new life and demonstrate that His purpose and plan for our lives are higher than human knowledge and wisdom. As we reflect on God and view His works in humankind, I am reminded of a family that had one daughter after the first year of marriage, and for several years it appeared that God had closed the mother's womb for nine years. The mother maintained they were trying to have another baby; but she did not conceive. Their one child wanted a baby brother because her cousins had sisters and brothers and she was an only child. Like Isaac who prayed for his wife to conceive, she prayed and asked God to give her a baby brother. Eventually, God answered her prayer and her mother conceived and birthed a boy. This was an answer to the little girl's prayer and she told everyone that God had given her a baby brother. Thirteen months later, the mother conceived again and bore a baby girl. Older sister, now 10 years old, told everybody she had prayed for one brother. From this family, I learned that God's design is to draw us into a closer relationship with Him and He will give us the desire of our heart and in some cases, He gives us more than we asked for. A little girl believed in the power of God to intervene and give her mother a baby boy. God was also concerned that her baby brother would have a baby sister nearer his age to play with since the older sister was ten years his senior.

Scriptural Verses Give Hope to Barren Women

Key verses in Scripture demonstrate the theological aspect of the barren wife motif. The Prophet Isaiah says, "*Sing, O barren one who did not bear; burst into song and shout, ...For the LORD has called you like a wife forsaken and grieved in spirit"* (Isaiah 54:1, 6).

The psalmist voice rings out the message of faith: *"He gives the barren woman a home, making her the joyous mother of children. Praise the Lord"* (Psalm 113:9).

The psalmist uses the barren wife motif as an example of God's power to invert the powerless. I Samuel 1:2, Hannah is an example of the inverted process. Although the contradiction refutes logical reasoning, Bruggemann says, "Every Israelite who sang this song would immediately pass in review the history of barrenness that has become well-being and fruitfulness" (*The Message of the Psalms*, p. 162). I have learned that singing in a barren situation gives praise to God, and the more I thank Him the less I feel sad and depressed. Barren matriarchs were very special women whose lives were closely connected to the service of a deity who cared for them and to whom, it seems, they had special access in times of need (*Sarah, the Priestess*, 106). Just as the matriarchs were chosen for special assignments by God to give birth to sons, I then began to see that God had a specific task for me to bring new life wherever He sent me to minister. Don't stop praying; call on God until you get an answer. Cry out to Him.

Ordinary Women Perform Extraordinary Work

As the Executive Pastor at the church where I was called to serve, I started a women's ministry group and we read a book entitled, *Journey to the Well* by Vashti McKenzie. The women's ministry began to grow spiritually in ways that can only be described as phenomenal. One lady in particular, took on more responsibility in the church, leading the fellowship committee, and serving on the committee to replace the carpet and refurbish the church for Easter. Ordinary women started performing extraordinary work as they were obedient to the leading of the Holy Spirit. After God brought new life in their lives, they began to do those things which they would not accept previously. I was so encouraged and inspired by reading the book that I began working on my book again - it had been put on the shelf and waiting to be completed. There was a power at work that we could not explain.

Barrenness is the Most Humiliating Experience for Hebrew Wives

Barren women were considered a curse and a social disgrace in their community, but God used the phenomenon of barrenness to show His divine provision. He gave Sarah a baby (the Promised Child) at ninety years of age. God gave Rebekah two boys after Isaac prayed. And God gave Rachel a son who became ruler over all Egypt and saved a nation from famine. Hannah gave birth to Samuel, Israel's first judge who was responsible for anointing two famous kings; and Manoah's wife (the only unnamed matriarch) gave birth to Samson who had extraordinary strength and defeated the Philistines. Even in the New Testament, God intervened and Elizabeth who was post-menopausal, conceived and gave birth to John the Baptist, the cousin and forerunner of the Son of God. And God sent an angel to a young virgin named Mary to announce that she would conceive a child by the Holy Spirit. She conceived the Son of God and gave birth to the Savior of the world.

Although barrenness is an inexplicable mystery, the phenomenon of barrenness is that God has timing and purpose that we don't understand. That's why it is a mystery to us. It seems to be one of God's own methods of bringing forth life at divinely appointed times. And the miracle is He brings glory to Himself, and the new personality can transform history. This is particularly evident in Israel's leadership during Samuel's prophecy, Joseph's reign as prime minister, and Samson's defeat of the Philistines; and after

Jacob wrestled with the Angel of the Lord, God changed his name to Israel.

Barrenness was more a divine matter of God's own timing than any physical inability to conceive a child. Some of the women and even their husbands understood this and knew God to be the Giver of life. In Genesis 25:21 we read, "Isaac prayed to the Lord for his wife, because she was barren; and the Lord granted his prayer, and Rebekah conceived." Abram was visited by three men at the plains of Mamre in Hebron while sitting under the trees (Genesis 18:10-14). While the men were talking with Abram, Sarai was listening to their conversation and heard the angel of the Lord telling Abram a message saying," I will surely return to you in due season, and your wife Sarai shall have a son" (Genesis 18:10). When Sarai heard what the angel said, she laughed because she was aware of the physical limitations that made it impossible for her to conceive a child. She was post-menopausal and Abram was one-hundred years old, but the Scriptures show, "By faith Abram and Sarai received power of procreation even though he was too old – and Sarai herself was barren – because he considered him faithful who had promised" (Hebrews 11:11). This same power worked hundreds of years later when Manoah entreated the Lord and prayed, "O Lord, I pray, let the man of God whom you sent come to us again and teach us what we are to do concerning the boy who will be born" (Judges 13:8). It should be noted that none of the patriarchs seemed to consider the possibility that the husband was sterile.

When Rachel demanded that Jacob give her children, Jacob reminded Rachel that he was not in the place of God who had closed her womb. One matriarch, Hannah, stands alone as a model of faith because she never doubted that she could conceive. She demonstrated her faith by what she did and did not do. Even after years of suffering from Penninah's taunting, Hannah did not use a handmaid as surrogate mother. Instead, she used the power of prayer to change her condition from barrenness to new life. Hannah responded in faith to her infertility by calling on the God of Israel to do for her what she desired, saying, "O Lord of hosts, if only you will look on the misery of your servant, and remember me, and not forget your servant, but will give to your servant a male child, then I will set him before you as a Nazarite until the day of his death" (I Samuel 1:11). Hannah did not consider that it was impossible for her to conceive a baby; she just talked about what God could do. Hannah did not put limitations on God's ability to give her a child.

Principles of Barrenness

Hannah prayed specifically about her condition, detailing what she wanted and also what she was willing to give back to God. First, she described her pain and suffering that all barren women experience when they desire to conceive a baby. Then she referred to herself three times as a servant of God and asked Him to remember her. Next, she petitioned God for a male child. Last, Hannah told God she was willing to give her child in consecrated service to the Lord, even before his birth. She prayed in accordance with God's will and purpose for her life. Hannah viewed her barren condition as a means of fulfilling a higher service as a servant of the Most High God. Hannah's prayer reminds us that our highest Christian duty is not what we can get from God, but what we can do and give in service that honors and brings glory to God, even the dedication and education of our offspring which are gifts from God.

The Significance of God Choosing Barren Women

There is a profound reason for God opening a closed womb after many years of barrenness. The reason is that a sovereign God desires to bring forth fruit in due season and that the miracle of childbirth may bring glory to Him and fulfill His own purpose and plan in the lives of His people. Each of the women of faith (Hannah and Manoah's wife) recognized that it is by divine providence, in spite of their limited physical ability, that their wombs were opened to produce new life. These foremothers of Israel believed in the power of God. They trusted Him to erase the years of misery and suffering, the disgrace of infertility, with His amazing grace. Miraculously, they each received the blessing of childbirth, after having been infertile for decades.

Five barren Hebrew matriarchs chosen, prepared and receptive vessels participated in God's Divine provisioning plan of birthing a leader for Israel during critical times in her history. The role patriarchs played was important to the unfolding drama and in interpreting and understanding the women's stories. In addition, I also introduce the topic regarding surrogacy and the moral question of whether to use Artificial Reproductive Therapy, a subject that Christian couples in today's society should discuss. These subjects are addressed in the following questions:

1. What is God's purpose for the matriarchs in Abraham's family giving birth after years of barrenness?
2. Who are the other barren matriarchs in the Hebrew Bible? What do they have in common with Abraham's family matriarchs?
3. How does each matriarch react to her individual condition of barrenness?
4. What is significant about God opening a matriarch's womb after many years of being barren? What is His purpose or plan for the child?
5. How do the problems of patriarchy help or hinder the interpretation of the story of barrenness?
6. What are the moral questions and dynamics regarding infertility and married couples seeking help through ART (Assisted Reproductive Therapy)?

Collected data was organized into categories and transferred to a matrix in order to study relevant themes, such as the wives' characteristics; and spiritual disciplines associated with the waiting process. The matrix helped to organize material that revealed other relevant categories: faith, waiting on God, and principles of fruitfulness. These new categories raised additional questions: what is the role of the patriarchs in interpreting the women's stories? And what do you say to married couples who may not become fertile? While counseling is beyond the scope of this book, the questions provided an opportunity to offer a chapter on "help and hope" for infertile couples.

Role of History and Humanity in the Barrenness Phenomenon

God choreographs the context of history through the shame and disgrace of barren women who were unaware of His plan, purpose and provision for their lives. The barren women had no idea of the plans and purposes God had for the babies they conceived and birthed. Thus, the place between the promise and the provision is a place of waiting in hope for new life.

But the uniqueness of this argument lies in the analysis of five sons whose births were inextricably tied to leadership during the most crucial times of Israel's history. God made each of the matriarchs fertile and miraculously opened a closed womb after decades of barrenness, even when one of the wives was post-menopausal.

The Hebrew Matriarchs and Why Were They Chosen

Sarai, Rebekah, Rachel, Hannah and Manoah's wife have similar stories that accurately portray the peculiarity in ancient Near East culture. Reviewing the literature published on Abram's family, Hannah and the unnamed wife of Manoah revealed strong character traits. Hannah was a woman of great faith and seemed to understand the purpose of her barrenness. She neither blamed her husband nor participated in surrogacy to cover her shame. Rather, Hannah sought God's help after years of being provoked by the rival wife. She really cried out to God in her heart while praying in the temple. Jewish men and women worshiped separately in the temple in Jerusalem and the women did not participate in Judaic religious life during Old Testament and New Testament times. Hannah was not standing beside her husband; no doubt other Jewish women were standing around her while she poured out her heart to God through weeping.

Theme of Barrenness in the Hebrew Bible

The theme of barrenness is woven throughout the chronicles of the Hebrew Bible. God promised to multiply Abram's seed, yet God's own promise seemed to be threatened and always at risk of dying out because all the matriarchs were barren for many years before God opened their wombs. It made me wonder, "What is God up to?" There must be a reason for all of these wives being barren. As a result of my questioning this recurring phenomenon in Scripture, this book also reveals the power of praying and trusting God for an answer to my barren condition.

God is bigger than our barren condition and He is able to deliver us from hopelessness to hopefulness on this spiritual journey and prepare us for His divine purpose. The words "less" and "full" have different meanings. Less means to have a smaller part and the suffix "less" means destitute or deprived. On the contrary, I would rather have "full" which means filled or having no empty or vacant space. The suffix "ness" means a state of being. Therefore, "hopefulness means a state of being in hope with no empty space." God is concerned about our human desires and our prayers do not go unheard. Sometimes He answers by telling us to wait, although the waiting seems in vain, but we wait in hope for the season to receive our blessing.

What is the Difference between the Promise and the Provision?

Learning to discern the difference between the promise and the provision prepares us for receiving fruit in our lives. God's timing and the manifestation of the blessing takes time just like the process of pregnancy takes nine months for a baby to grow in the mother's womb. After birth, it takes years of nurturing the baby to grow into maturity. Cultivating a relationship with God can prepare us for the miraculous things He wants to do in our lives. Just as the matriarch's desired a baby, God's desire was for the matriarchs to trust Him fully. God is concerned about divine provision for Israel and His provision for their future. God sees our future. Human problems arise in bringing the provision to fruition, such as the patriarchal problems that placed the matriarch in a precarious position, especially when they made unwise decisions to act in ways that show self-preservation over the welfare of a spouse. Acts of disobedience to God also caused problems.

Barrenness was more than a physical problem as we learn from Hannah's prayer life; barrenness can be a spiritual condition as well. Barrenness as a spiritual condition shows us that we need to draw closer to God in prayer and be receptive to the Holy Spirit to give us the new life. Our human efforts alone, no matter how smart or powerful or connected, will not bring about the desire of our hearts.

Stories of laments and protests reveal some of the patriarchs' problems as well, especially how they responded to the occurrence of barrenness. In Abram's family, barrenness was about multiplying the covenant seed for the Nation. Both historical and spiritual contexts of the five Hebrew matriarchs are emphasized because each of the matriarchs gave birth to a son who became a leader in Israel's history according to God's plan for their lives.

God's Sovereignty in Timing the Birth of Israel's Leaders

Sons born miraculously through barren wombs will not only multiply Abram's seed and fulfill God's divine plan, but they will provide leadership for the Nation of Israel. That is the uniqueness of this book -- God uses barrenness to draw special attention toward women who seem to be a disgrace and a shame in a community, yet actually serve as chosen vessels in birthing a child who brings glory to Him. These women are not in the limelight or historical figures. As Cain Hope Felder emphasizes, "Irrespective of their social position, some Old Testament women who at first appear to be of low estate later attain great theological significance by liberating themselves from their circumstances and participating dramatically in God's redemptive plan" (*Troubling Biblical Waters*, 141). I try to answer the question, "What does one need to do on their spiritual journey from barrenness to become fruitful?"

Knowing When to Move On

In her book, *Reading the New Testament*, Pheme Perkins describes the "Divisions of Jesus' Ministry." Perkins shows in Luke's gospel that Jesus was rejected at Nazareth (4:22-29), Samaria (9:52-56) and Jerusalem (19:42-48). Other gospel writers also show what Jesus did when He experienced rejection (Mark 6:1-14; John 4:30; 8:59 and 10:39). Notice, Jesus was rejected at the place where people knew Him, His hometown, including the place of worship, and the synagogue. But Jesus did not give up and throw in the towel because He knew that God had sent Him on a mission to preach, teach and heal those who are broken in spirit and body.

A distinct difference exists between those who accept Jesus and His ministry and those who reject Him. Jesus is our model for what we must do in times of rejection. If we follow His example, notice that Jesus went His way. He went to a familiar place beyond the Jordan where He had been baptized by John. Jesus moved on when He was rejected. That's what we must do; move on to another place where people will accept us with joy. Rejection may signal a message that it is time for you to move on.

Knowing when to move on is the key to beginning the ministry God has called you to do. When is the right time to move on? When doors are closed that used to be open; that's a sign it is time to move on. When I served as an interim minister, the doors were open for five years. I had no problem getting a position because the door of opportunity was open for me. But years later when I applied for positions and was rejected, it was not immediately clear to me that the door of opportunity for that ministry was shut. I began to pray that God would show me what He wanted me to do. The answer to me - it is time to move on - God was opening another door. When I walked through the new door, which I had not applied for, it allowed me to work from home and use my gifts of teaching in another venue. I did not have to travel miles from home to get another position.

What's more important, I served a much larger population through writing than I could ever have reached in a parish setting. Writing Christian articles, Sunday school lessons and teacher guides for Vacation Bible School provided another avenue of ministering to the body of Christ. God also provided another place to teach and preach. Then I recalled the words a mentor and friend had spoken to me many years ago when I first started in interim ministry, she said, "God has a place for you." Some unforgettable words - spoken by Dr. Kortright

Davis, professor at Howard University Divinity School told us in class one day - "The God who calls is the same God who prepares and the same God who sends." Those two sentences have remained with me for many years and I believe God used both of them to encourage me in the barren times to know that He is the same God who called me and that He has a place for me in ministry.

Reflection Questions:

1. Have you experienced rejection in your ministry?
2. How will you know when God is speaking to you about moving on? What are the signs?

Discussion Question/Topic:

1. What will you notice happening to you in places where you are known and by people who are familiar with your ministry?
2. Tell a partner what you learned about the difference in physical barrenness and spiritual barrenness.

NOTES

Queen Makeda's Journey

Queen Makeda who was also known as the Queen of Sheba reigned over parts of Southern Arabia. She heard about the fame concerning King Solomon and wanted to question him with hard questions to learn whether he had the giftedness that others had proclaimed. Queen Makeda journeyed to Jerusalem seeking to hear the wisdom of the king. According to the book entitled, *The Kebra Nagat*, Queen Makeda said, "The report I heard in my own country about your achievements and your wisdom is true. But I did not believe these things until I came and saw with my own eyes" (I Kings 10:6-7NIV). In Queen Makeda's memoirs, it is reported that she worshipped the sun god, but she also glorified the God who blessed Solomon. She wrote in her memoirs, "Praise be to the Lord your God, who has delighted in you and placed you on the throne of Israel. Because of the Lord's eternal love for Israel, he has made you king, to maintain justice and righteousness" (I Kings 10:9NIV).

She journeyed to Jerusalem seeking to hear the wisdom of a king, but Queen Makeda learned more than King Solomon's wisdom -- she received the wisdom of God and returned as a worshipper of the God of Israel (Matthew 12:42).

CHAPTER THREE

The Post Reviews Of Journey Literature

Many scholars have delved into the Scriptures and written volumes that have been published on the subject of barrenness. Review of the literature includes current research studies about the women's lives in ancient Israel and their roles as mothers and wives. Journal articles look at the mythological aspect of barrenness in the Hebrew Bible as well as thoughts related to the sociological perspectives of identity and ideology, two areas that touch a barren woman's life. Since barrenness touches a woman in many dimensions; it cannot be measured in just one aspect of life. Because men were allowed to have more than one legal wife, there was yet another dimension to the matriarch wife's role in marriage. For a barren wife, this can be a very precarious relationship, since "A woman was a second-class citizen valued as an asset in procreation" (*Journey to the Well*, 94). Rachel and Hannah are two wives who have this unusual relationship with a rival child-bearing wife.

A Mistress, a Maid, and No Mercy

As mentioned above, one of the characteristics of the barren matriarch is her self-image in the community. In

Just a Sister Away (1988), Renita Weems delves into Sarai's description in Genesis 16:1. The Bible describes Sarai by her status as the wife of Abram, her social position shows that she also had an Egyptian handmaid, but her human condition shows that she bore no child. That's the sum of Sarai's status, a wife with no children in an ancient Near East community which valued large families. In the twenty-first century, women have different value systems - they are varied depending on education, background, family and vocation – which may surround family, work, education or community. Weems suggests, "In ancient times a woman's self-worth and social status pivoted around her family – namely the reputation of her husband and, more importantly, the number of children she had borne, preferably males" (2).

Although God had promised to bless Abram and Sarai with a child in His covenant agreement (Genesis 17:5-17), Weems says Sarai was "too impatient to trust God's promise to her husband" (12). In her impatience, Sarai "lost sight of who she was in relation to the sovereign Word of God" (12); no doubt, impatience was due to how she viewed herself as a childless wife in a community of large families. Israel's economy depended upon male heirs in the family. Losing sight of her relationship to God and His promise, Sarai was not only physically barren, she was spiritually barren. Sometimes a woman may opt to use the methods suggested by culture instead of waiting on God's timing. Barrenness teaches us to seek God's answer and to wait for His timing.

Rabbinic Reflections on the Barren Wife

Judith R. Baskin (1989) in her article on reflections on barren women represents "insights into the dilemma of suffering, the efficacy of prayer, as well as examples of biblical models that could become paradigms and symbols of empowerment in women's lives" (101). Baskin suggests that rabbinic literature shows compassion for the childless and hesitates to explain the divine dispensation in an easy manner. Baskin says, "There is an interesting homiletical trend to reinterpret verses traditionally understood to refer to infertility in alternate ways" (108). Psalm 55:19 and Deuteronomy 7:14 support her viewpoint. Baskin's reflections on the special insights into rabbinic views of barrenness can also be derived from the midrashic traditions about each barren biblical couple (113). According to Baskin, the "barren wife doubtless felt great shame and endured reproach for disappointing her husband at home and in the eyes of the world" (109), based on rabbinic exegeses of the biblical literature. Baskin argues that Rabbis were aware of (women's) pain evidenced by their interpretation of scriptures (Genesis 30:22-23; Genesis 16:2, 4). In Genesis 30:22 and 16:2, Sarai and Rachel both felt the shame and disgrace of barrenness.

Barren Woman

In "Barren Woman" (*Women in Scripture*, 2000), Carol Meyers focuses her discussion on "Ancient Israel's agrarian economy" and "childless women who are considered marginal because they do not contribute to society and their families" (199-200). Meyers noted that "pregnant women represented survival."

Meyers claims in her essay, "Everyday Life" (*Women's Bible Commentary*, 255) that "The reason why barren matriarchs felt the weight of the curse is because Ancient Israel's economy depended on large families". Meyers also explains that the economic system was the driving force that necessitated "the continued life of the community as well as the survival of individual families depended upon female fertility" (199). Other biblical scholars who have interpreted barrenness in relation to how suffering produces prayer in the barren matriarch agree with Meyers (Dresner, 1991; Ashmon and Weise, 1998).

Hebrew Scripture, for example, Exodus 23:26 says "God promises the absence of barrenness when the Israelites are faithful to their God" and Deuteronomy 7:14 says, "There shall not be male or female barren among you, or among your cattle." Poetic language in Scripture also speaks to the barren wife motif in descriptive Psalms of praise. The psalmist exalts God when he says, in Psalm 113:9, "He makes the barren woman to keep house and be a joyful mother of children." He speaks of God using His creative power to lift up the powerless, the barren woman who feels like a "social outcast". God says that the barren woman will celebrate new fertility after the Exile (Isaiah 54:1), which is a "dawn of the New Age". New life comes whenever God promises to pour out His Spirit on all flesh (Joel 2:28). The prophet Isaiah also prophesied about a time when the church would be enlarged due to barren women giving birth. So God has promised new life, not only for the church but for barren women, too.

Woman as Oppressed, Woman as Liberated in Scriptures

Rosemary Radford Ruether unveils the subject of oppression and liberation of the barren woman motif and how the barren woman viewed herself (her essay in *Spinning a Sacred Yarn*, 1983). Her study revealed the depth of the internalized oppression of barren wives, that gave Hannah the ability to voice her pain and suffering by revealing her inner feelings in prayer and supplication. Notice, Hannah's *voice* was not heard in her prayer and meditation in the temple, nevertheless, God heard her deep sighing and moaning for deliverance. Although Hannah only moved her lips, God heard the longing cries for a baby. Ruether notices the difference in Hannah's hymn after her meeting with the priest. Eli thought she was drunk. Hannah begins her hymn with gratitude, praise and rejoicing in the Lord and exalting His awesome power. Then she emphasizes His power, noting He makes the weak strong and the strong weak -- reversal by His awesome power. The one, who was called barren, speaks prophetically of more children. She recognizes that God has the power to reverse the fortunes of the rich and poor. This remarkable woman's prayer became a hymn of exaltation and thanksgiving echoed in Mary's Magnificat. When you experience the transformative power of God's reversal in your situation, then you, too, will rejoice with Hannah in praise.

God's action in delivering Hannah's oppression is a symbol of Israel's and her redemption. Hannah's continued prayer is spoken centuries later by a young teen-age girl who also connects with the Old Testament hymn. Mary's connection with Hannah's hymn demonstrates that barren women no longer have to be redeemed by bearing a male child. Mary becomes a new paradigm and symbol of empowerment for women. She was not barren, but heard the Word of God and received the gift of promise through faith. Mary conceived not by human contact with a man, but by the power of the Holy Spirit.

Heroic Barrenness in the Hebrew Bible

The movement from barrenness to conception and birth is shown through the stories of Jacob and Rachel in Genesis, chapter 29 verses 31 through chapter 30, verse 24. We notice God's providential hand in the movement which is not accomplished by human action. In her essay, Rachel Havrelock (2008) introduces the concept of the hero pattern, where "movement from barrenness to fertility is a mode of female initiation into a relationship with the divine" (154). On one hand, Havrelock focuses attention on the mother's actions; specifically protest, showing barren women who make a statement of protest either to God or their husbands

(162-164) set a course for action. Women need to make a protest, but they need to focus on articulating their pain rather than focusing on the persons or institutions that cause the pain.

Havrelock's suggested seven steps may have merit for some women to overcome their barrenness through learning to pray about their condition. She proposes that there is "the infinity between the birthing stories and suggests that the meaning of the barrenness motif is generated through this interrelationship" (159). Her argument for partnership with God is a movement from barrenness to fertility. The emphasis should be on Hannah's action with Elkanah after returning home from Shiloh. She participated in her own deliverance demonstrating that Hannah forged a relationship with God and with her husband after her prayer was heard in the temple.

Barren women who bridged the gap between infertility, conceiving and birthing a child, forged a relationship with God through prayer: Hannah's specific prayer for a man child and Rebekah's prayer questioning God about her condition, both began a relationship with God. Sarai, on the other hand, laughed when she heard the stranger tell Abram that she would conceive and bear a son. But I hasten to add, it was through Sarai's dialogue and her relationship with the Lord that Sarai received the faith to believe she could conceive (Hebrews 11:11). Havrelock maintains that miraculous births require a partnership between a woman and the Creator as well as a sexual union between a woman and a man (174). Havrelock maintains, "God's involvement in the equation suggests that it is not human coupling alone that result in conception" (174). The miraculous births are not to be confused with the virgin birth. There are three matriarchs who specifically speak of having sexual relations with their husbands. Sarai talks about "having pleasure" with her husband in their old age; Rachel wants to try Mandrakes to aid her fertility when she has sex with Jacob. Hannah's action demonstrates the principle of this equation "Elkanah knew his wife." Partnership between the Creator and with their husbands was seemingly understood by these matriarchs.

Barrenness in the Old Testament: Recovering the Metaphor

In her poignant discussion of women's lives in Ancient Israel and their roles as mothers and wives in the community, Sarah Derck (2002) states, "A woman's identity, both within her own heart and mind and in the eyes of others was in her motherhood" (4). Derck touches the lives of many infertile women who have these same concepts of her self-image in the community that is shaped by the "experiences of barrenness with emotions of yearnings and unfulfillment, and perhaps even worthlessness" (10). Sarah Derck's emphasis on recovering the metaphor of barrenness touches the nerve center of the problem of barrenness in the Christian church. One needs to understand the dynamics of feeling barren in different situations.

As a minister, I felt barren when I received rejection letters from Search Committees for pastoral positions where I had applied. After serving as an interim minister for several years, I began seeking a full-time pastoral position; it was very painful to be denied an opportunity to serve. The rejection letters were just as painful to read as the woman who hears from her doctor that she is infertile. At some point in our lives all of us experience barrenness in some form. Some people may feel rejection on the job when someone else receives the promotion that you had applied for; some may feel rejection when you apply for a college that you wanted to attend and was turned down. Rejection may come in marriage when one mate asks for divorce.

Sarah Derck's thought-provoking message of restoring the experience of barrenness to the faith community to recover the metaphor in barrenness could be used as a teaching tool to help women and men recover from their physical and spiritual barrenness. Derck suggests:

> We recognize opportunities and pronouncements of physical barrenness in the Old Testament (to) serve as a point of connection for ministry opportunities. There is a need for recognition of despair and bitterness, hope and joy as a stimulus for recognition of those experiences in our own relations with people (94).

Each of these areas requires healing of our spiritual, relational and mental selves. The first step is to acknowledge our hurts and ask God to touch us in those places that no one can see. Share in the suffering of barrenness. This does not mean to remove disgrace; rather, it offers God's grace to others who are suffering from a barren condition. According to Sarah Derck, "Every human being experiences barrenness in one way or another: barrenness of the soul, of the conscience, of the spirit" (94).

By examining the barrenness narratives as a background for one of Israel's theological expressions of blessings, we too, may be blessed and experience healing. The theme of barrenness allows us to tap into our own grief stories "To reclaim the experience of barrenness for the church, forming a body of faith with a well-rounded understanding of the plight of barren families, and liberating those who suffer to share their pain and faith with the family of Christ" (95).

The Beautiful and the Barren

James Williams (1980) provides an interesting enlightenment on separation of beauty and barrenness in his article entitled, "The Beautiful and the Barren." He discusses the use of literary conventions to tell and reshape favorite biblical stories focusing on four type-scenes. Williams's notes "beauty is a theme that can be associated with fertility" (115). Beauty is an outward physical feature which has nothing to do with fertility or blessing. Also, there is beauty that goes beyond the physical appearance; it can be a special grace or charm. The favorite wives, Sarai, Rebekah, Rachel and Hannah, are barren and beautiful. However, Williams points out "The matriarch is never described as beautiful in the barrenness configuration" (115): Genesis 18, Genesis 29:31-30:24 and Genesis 25:19-26, respectively for Sarai, Rachel and Rebekah. There are "certain type-scenes, requiring or allowing certain conventions, elaborations and innovations but excluding others" (115). According to Williams, "The beauty configuration is centered in the potential of fertility and blessedness (and that) beauty is a code that the mother is blessed and a cue that her progeny will be favored" (115).

As a result, themes of beauty and barrenness are kept separate but they provide dramatic tension in the drama of the desired child (116). Sarai's beauty is one of the reasons that Abraham lied to the King about their relationship. Outward beauty plays a negative role which has nothing to do with fertility or blessing. Williams concludes, "If beauty is a sign of favor with God and potential fertility, barrenness is a sign of actual sterility - until God intervenes" (116). When God intervenes He does something *beautiful* with their lives that the outward beauty could not accomplish. He further states, "If the mother could give birth 'naturally', then the origins of her progeny would not be sacred. God is the one who opens and closes wombs".

Sing, O Barren One

In her notable book entitled, *Sing, O Barren One: A Study in Comparative Midrash* (1986), Mary Callaway developed the barren matriarch tradition in a chapter highlighting three points and noted the similarity of five barren matriarchs' stories that contain birth narratives for Sarah, Rebekah, Rachel, Manoah's wife and Hannah. Callaway uses the Scriptures from Second Isaiah (Isaiah 49:19-21; 51:1-3; and 54:1-3) to support her position and she focuses on symbolic representation of the barren matriarch. Her statement, "The barren matriarch is a symbol of the people rather than an individual woman" is quite creative. It provided a new lens to view the barren matriarch's importance as God had designed. Callaway noted the Exile experience to interpret a new form of barren matriarch tradition as a new transformation (59). Indeed, Callaway's insightful argument provided a new structure of how Israel defined herself in the Second Temple period (60). On one hand, the text shifts from a birth narrative of a child to a message focusing on the mother. This shifting signals a new purpose for the future (63-64). But she also demonstrates how God uses the barren mother and the eventual son for future leadership, which is the main focus on this book.

Callaway emphasizes that Second Isaiah combined two traditions: (1) ancient mythological, the birth of the first man; and (2) the historical, the birth of Isaac that results in an image of creation of Israel from the first parents. God chose barren Sarah, through this new creation, to become the mother of all Israel (60) in Isaiah 54:1. The unnamed Zion, as she was identified in Isaiah 49:19-21, is a figure for the "whole people Israel" (64). Thus demonstrating how the story of Sarah's barrenness was interpreted in Isaiah 54:1-3 as a personification of Jerusalem, the wife of the deity. By emphasizing God's gift of children to Sarah, Second Isaiah reinterprets the promise of making a people through a 90-year-old barren wife and 100-year-old Abram. However, the main focus was barren Sarai, rather than wealthy land-owner Abram.

Notice how Second Isaiah (Isaiah 54:2) uses the story of Abram and Sarai as a reference to the gift of children to Sarai, and the story is told at Abram's tent. The place where he pitched his tent and worshipped God, is the place of waiting on God (Genesis 13:18). The same place where Abram receives God's reassurance of the Promised Child is significant because Abram liked to build altars to worship and remember God's help. The same place where the divine provision is made is the same place that prompts my praise for what God is doing in my life. The place of receiving the blessing reassures me that God is working on my behalf. The place that is holy ground where an altar is built to remember God keeps His promises. Callaway highlights reinterpreting the promise through aged parents. I suggest that remembering the place where the future parents received the message is most important.

The writer of Second Isaiah notes the necessity of enlarging the family tent in relation to the discussion and anticipation of more children because the dwelling place is where the mother will nurture the Promised Child. Therefore, the message that Sarai will have a son is given to Abram at the tent entrance is also significant. The Lord appears to Abram when three visitors come to his tent, located by the oaks of Mamre (Genesis 18:1). Abram told the visitors that Sarai was in the tent (Genesis 18:9), and one of them announces that Sarai will give birth to a son in due season. Listening to the whole conversation and laughing to herself (at the thought of conceiving a child), is Sarai standing behind them at the tent entrance (Genesis 18:10). What an impossibility she thought!

Although Abram is the one who receives the message, the emphasis is on Sarai and not her husband. However, the message is in accordance with the promise of abundance of descendants (Genesis 17:2). The identity of the postexilic community as children of the promise obtained in Babylon further emphasizes that God keeps His promise to multiply Abram's seed, illustrating that God's focus is on the children of the promise (72). God promised to multiply Abram's seed: "A woman can give birth anywhere; Yahweh can build up his people wherever a contemporary Sarah and Abraham are living" (72).

Hannah's Desire, God's Design

Joan Cook (1999) weaves the barren mother stories' themes (10) and depicts Hannah as a catalyst for reform on the "priesthood and creation of the monarchy" (9). Cook uses adaptations from three sources to design barren mother models[1] with descriptions for each type. Cook's general descriptions of a "biblical barren mother type is a childless woman who bears a son through divine intervention, then takes steps to ensure her son's success" (10). Cook's analysis: "Often the sons in question serve a special function as leaders of the people in times of crisis or transition" (10). She introduces three barren mother types along with characteristics of the barren mother that fits each model and the categories are extremely helpful. The Shumnamite woman does not fit models that I have outlined in this book because her son does not become one of Israel's leaders. Cook's descriptions of three barren mother models are:

1. *The Competition Model* which includes Sarah, Rachel and Hannah. All three women are the favored wife.

---

1   R. Alter in *The Art of Biblical Narrative* (New York: Basic Books, 1981), 49, 85. J.G. Williams in *Women Recounted: Narrative Thinking and the God of Israel* (Sheffield: Almond Press, 1982), 48-55. A. Brenner in *The Israelite Woman: Social Role and Literacy Type* in *Biblical Narrative* (Sheffield: Journal of the Study of Old Testament Press, 1985), 92-95.

And the other wife bears a son and the rival wife belittles the childless wife, causing conflict. The five elements of the *Competition Model* are:

a. favored wife; husband has another wife, rival woman;

b. the rival bears a son for the husband;

c. the rival belittles the childless wife, causing difficulty;

d. the childless wife bears a son through divine intervention; and

e. the child receives a significant name. (14-15)

2. The *Promise Model* includes Sarah, Manoah's wife, and Hannah. In this model, a messenger from God appears and promises a son; the son is born and receives a significant name. It is important to note who receives a visit with the promise from the messenger of God; Abraham, not Sarah, receives three promises (Genesis 15:4; 17:15-19; 18:9-15). The angel of the Lord appeared to Manoah's wife and told her that she would bear a son who would begin to deliver Israel from the Philistines (Judges 13:3-5). In Hannah's case, she makes the promise by vowing to give back to God the son she prays for (I Samuel 1:11). And Hannah names her son, Samuel which means "I have asked him of the Lord". The five elements in this model include:

a. the wife is childless;

b. a messenger from God appears to one or the other spouse

c. the messenger promises a son

d. the event is confirmed despite human doubt

e. the promised son is born and receives a significant name. (14, 17)

3. The *Request Model* includes Rebekah, Rachel and Hannah. In this model Isaac prays to God for his wife Rebekah, she conceives and has twins who begin fighting in the womb before birth. After birth they continue fighting for the birthright. Rachel's request is made to her husband in the form of a demand that he give her children. Hannah goes to the temple and makes a public and formal plea in the form of a vow (I Samuel 1:9-11). The model consists of a simple plot with only three elements:
   a. someone requests a son for a barren wife
   b. the Lord hears the request
   c. a son is given (15,18-19)

Dedicated women who take the initiative for themselves and their families to ensure the blessing of a son demonstrate strong character. When Hannah finds her voice she makes her petition to God for a son. Before Hannah found her voice, the only sound she made was her weeping whenever she was provoked by her rival, Penninah.

Hannah's noteworthy characteristics of competition, promise and request are highlighted (14-15) in the competition model. Hannah faces belittling from Penninah; she is "distressed, (yet) she does not respond to Penninah's teasing" (I Samuel 1:6-7). Moreover, Hannah does not even respond to her husband who seemingly does not understand her grief (I Samuel 1:8). When falsely accused by Eli of being drunk, Hannah described her condition as an affliction (that can be healed); she was grief-stricken with a sorrowful spirit. But after praying to God and receiving the priest's blessing, she went home with a different countenance and a renewed mind and spirit because she believed God would answer her petition.

The scriptures show that both human initiative and divine purpose is Hannah's model of partnering with God and her husband. Hannah shows dignity instead of bitterness. She elevated her petition above the taunting and teasing from Penninah and seeks God's deliverance. And through divine intervention, she conceived and bore a son. Her prayer focused on God's power to deliver her from oppression as a symbol of Israel's redemption as well as Hannah's (183). Ruether affirms, "God does not give Hannah a child through a 'virgin birth,' but by acting within the natural sexual intercourse of Hannah and Elkanah" (183). God can give new life in barren situations. She acted on the Word of promise from the priest (I Samuel 1:17) and placed her faith in God's power to receive her blessing. We, too, must be participants in our deliverance and healing.

Give Me Children, or I Will Die: Procreation Is God's Work

Scott Ashmon and Robert Weise (1998) provide a different point of view as they discuss the subject of barrenness. They introduce methods of our culture that provide a remedy without a partnership with God. Using the twentieth century medical term "infertility" Ashmon and Weise cite work done in the nineties where barren couples opt for methods called ART (Assisted Reproductive Technology) to have a baby. ART refers to all techniques. There are seven ART techniques listed, along with their explanations. Moral questions for Christian couples to explore are explained in Chapter Six, "Infertility: Help and Hope for Married Couples."

Under professional consultation with a physician or a specialist in the field of obstetrics and gynecology, infertile couples receive guidance about treatment and therapy methods (*Infertility: Understanding a Complex Condition*, 4). Knowing the options and all aspects of treatments can be very helpful in diagnosing and educating yourself about infertility. According to Dr. Marcia Watson-Whitmyre, "Some women have hormonal difficulties that can be treated successfully with so-called fertility drugs."[2] The methods are:

1. Fertility drugs, a treatment for women with hormonal difficulties
2. Artificial insemination, a previously collected sperm sample is placed in the woman's vagina or uterus with a special tube
3. Gamete intra-fallopian transfer (GIFT), a surgical placement of ova and sperm into the woman's oviducts
4. In vitro fertilization (IVF), known as the "test-tube baby" technique; useful for women who are infertile because of endometriosis
5. Embryo freezing, doctors collect ova and combine with the sperm for fertilization; extra embryos can be frozen for later use, if the first ones implanted in the uterus do not survive
6. Nonsurgical embryo transfer, a fertile woman is artificially inseminated at the time of ovulation, five days later, her uterus is flushed with a sterile solution, washing out the resulting embryo before it implants in the uterus; the retrieved embryo is transferred to the uterus in another woman to carry it to full term.
7. Surrogate, a woman who agrees to bear a child and turn it over to the infertile couple to rear as their own; the surrogate is artificially inseminated with the sperm of the infertile woman's husband.[3]

---

2   http://elibrary.bigchalk.com: *Report on Infertility: Female Disease/Disorder,* Editors of Salem Press: Magill's Medical Guide, 4th Rev. Ed., 12-01-2008.

3   Marcia Watson-Whitmyre, *Infertility: Female, Disease/ Disorder,* Salem PressMagill's Medical Guide, 5th Rev. 12-01-2009;   http://elibrary.bigchalk.com/elibweb/elib/do/ document:set=search&groupid=1&request.

However, "each ART method uses donor sperm or egg or a surrogate mother" (337). Ashmon and Weise describe a barren wife's suffering and frustration, along with another key component, the sociological aspect (Sarah Derck, 2002; Meyers, 2000) that Hebrew women experienced in their community as the driving force for women to use ART.

Ashmon and Weise argue against using ART as a means of having a baby citing scriptural cases that show "textual" disclosure against surrogacy (340). They maintain that God is in control of infertility and that those who prayed to God, He intervened and they conceived.

In fact, Ashmon and Weise cite those who prayed to God in scripture: Hannah (I Samuel 1:2, 5-6); Isaac prayed for Rebekah (Genesis 25:21); and Zechariah prayed for Elizabeth (Luke 1:7, 13, 5-7). God promised Abram that Sarai would have a son, but when Sarai became impatient and used Hagar as a surrogate, God brings contempt and division between Hagar and Sarah (Genesis 16:3).

Ashmon and Weise argue that God is against methods of circumventing His method of producing children other than procreation through marital sexual union. While I believe that God answers prayer, and that we should wait on His answer, God also gives us guidance and direction to seek the answer we are looking for from those He has prepared to help us. That's why I believe it is so important for Christian, married couples to be in prayer and discussions with a spiritual advisor before making decisions about the use of ART.

Barren Rachel

Samuel H. Dresner (1991) describes why a woman felt the pain and suffering of barrenness so intensely. Dresner explains that oppression was felt on three levels by barren women: "barrenness as a woman is one thing, as a Hebrew woman is another, but to the barren as a matriarch adds a further dimension." Each level signals another dimension of oppression for the matriarch which means that the pain was compiled. The first dimension signifies natural order, the second Divine purpose, while the third suggests the assurance of the covenant. Dresner states the importance of these levels is according to the Covenant God made with Abraham. He states:

> The covenant promised blessing to all mankind through the people that would come from Abraham and Sarah. But without a child, there could be no people, and without the people no blessing for mankind. It was the bearing of a successor-child that represented fulfillment of the matriarchal role (446).

Because the matriarch felt shame and disgrace on three levels, the wife who did not fulfill her matriarchal role was considered a marginal woman. Dresner notes, "though these barren matriarchs were the favorites of husbands who never berated them for their state, they continue to berate themselves as incomplete, as fostering a kind of death within life" (447). Consider Jacob's wife, Rachel: "Rachel wants to be not only a wife, but a mother...She feels unfulfilled on all three levels: as a woman, as a Hebrew, and a matriarch" (448). Rachel's plaintive cry, "Give me children, or else I die", can be understood when we view her deep pain and suffering through the prism of physically dying unless she bears a child to fulfill her three dimensional roles: as a woman, a Hebrew woman and matriarch. As we consider the depth of pain and heartache of barren women and relate it to our situation, we are able to tap into our own stories of grief and pain (Cook, 1999; Ruether, 1983; and Dresner, 1991). Cook, Dresner and Ruether are right in their observations of how the barrenness theme can become a catalyst for ministers to share in others' painful experiences and become change agents and ministers of compassion to hurting humanity.

Reflection Questions:

1. Which one of the wives do you relate to and why? Share your praise report with a partner.
2. How are the barren matriarchs' stories similar to or different from your spiritual journey?
3. Do you know anyone who was barren, prayed to God and then conceived a baby?
   Share the story of their experience with a group or partner.
4. Close this session with prayer for each other and the women that you discussed.

NOTES

Naomi's Journeys

There was a famine in the land of Bethlehem, therefore, Naomi took her first journey with her husband and two sons to a country that lay along the east side of the Dead Sea, called Moab (Ruth 1:1). While they were living in Moab, Naomi's husband died first and then her two sons (who had married Moabite women) also died leaving her a widow without any means of support (Ruth 1:2-5). Later, Naomi heard that there was food back in Bethlehem and she decides to return to her homeland. And her two daughters-in-law (Ruth and Orpah) decided to return with her. Naomi tried to persuade them to turn back to Moab to live with their mother, and Orpah listened to her advice and went back to her people, but Ruth clung to Naomi.

Then Naomi blessed and kissed Orpah as they separated (Ruth 1:14). Vowing to go wherever Naomi went and to stay with her until death, Ruth (Ruth 1:16) accompanied Naomi on the pilgrimage to Bethlehem. These two women journeyed together around the Dead Sea until they come to Bethlehem which some commentators say is "the lowest point on earth."

When they arrived in Bethlehem, it was the beginning of the barley season. All the townspeople came out to greet her because they were delighted to see Naomi again. But Naomi asked them not to call her Naomi which means *Pleasant*, she said call me *Mara* which means *Bitter* (Ruth 1:20).

Naomi claimed that she was full when she left Bethlehem. And she believed the Lord had dealt harshly with her and brought her back empty (Ruth 1:21). Is it possible that the perception Naomi had of her circumstance could be the cause of the pain she experienced in losing a husband and two sons? When we view Naomi's spiritual journey (from married life to widowhood) and how it changed her perception of herself, it appears that her movements from famine to plenty caused her to see herself in a negative light. Naomi felt full when she had a husband and two sons, even though there was a famine in Bethlehem. But she described herself as empty when she returned to Bethlehem (a place that had become plentiful). She had a devoted daughter-in-law who returned with her and not only vowed to stay with her forever, but she left her own mother and family back in Moab. It seems as though Naomi based her perception on how she felt according to the people who were in her life, not on the God who remained the same. The location of Bethlehem did not change, but the condition of Bethlehem changed from famine to plenty. God had not changed. I believe that Naomi's spiritual journeys can be instructive for us. God is always our means of support; He is the One who is our provision in times of famine and plenty. Whenever one source of support dries up and is taken away, God provides new resources from unexpected people and places.

CHAPTER FOUR

The Personal Testimonies And Narratives Of Barren Wives

◇◇◇◇◇

Those who have been through a test have a testimony to give – these heart-felt stories, narratives, and prayers provide a glimpse into the lives of the barren women's experiences. Only one wife used some form of assisted reproductive technology (ART). These biblical and twenty-first century women have one thing in common; they were all barren. But they conceived and birthed a baby.

Laughing with Sarah

My name is Sarah and this is my testimony about what happened when I heard the angel of the Lord tell my husband, Abram, that I would become a mother at the age of ninety. I was listening at the tent entrance behind the curtain, and out of sight when three men visited my husband and talked with him by the oak trees. I thought no one would see or hear me, so I laughed to myself at what I heard one of them say. Me, a ninety-year old woman going to have a baby next year! Laughter was my only outburst, it released the amazement that I felt - mixed with joy and happiness. I didn't know whether to cry or laugh, but laughter seemed more appropriate at what I had heard.

Once I felt despair because of my aged and withered body. Now, I heard one of the men say that God was going to open my womb and give me a baby, just when I thought all hope was gone. For many years I tried to cover my shame of being barren by giving my handmaid (Hagar) to Abram to have a child. But God had made a covenant with my husband (Genesis 17:1-4) and told him that a child would come through my womb (Genesis 17:15-19). I didn't know it then, but when God makes a promise, He keeps it. To mark the time of the promise, God changed my husband's name from Abram to Abraham and He changed my name from Sarai to Sarah (Genesis 17:5, 15). At that time, both of us laughed at God because we thought it was ludicrous for me to conceive a child when I was so far past childbearing years. But God gave me strength to conceive a baby in my old age (Romans 9:8). And now, everyone can laugh with me.

A Narrative about Sarah and Laughter

The Apostle Paul later says of the Israelites, "Now you, my friends, are children of the promise, like Isaac" (Galatians 4:28). Although Sarai laughed at the promise, she birthed Isaac, the "Promised Child" who was born after the Spirit; thus, fulfilling the divine promise. The Apostle Paul identifies Sarah as the mother of "Children of Promise" (*Women in Scripture*, Meyers, 152). Paul later says, "For this is the word of promise, at this time will I come and Sarai shall have a son" (Romans 9:9).

Sarah's story is a lesson in developing a faith walk with God, from impatience to spiritual maturity and knowing that even in old age, God can still perform inexplicable miracles. We learn that "God is adamant...only Sarai can give birth to the child of the covenant" (Trible, 42). Thus, we can believe in God's power to deliver from the stigma of disgrace no matter how long it takes for Him to answer prayer. Although

God's timing may seem to be late in the natural realm, Sarah's testimony confirms: "Through faith also Sarai herself received strength to conceive seed, and was delivered of a child when she was past age, because she judged him faithful who had promised" (Hebrews 11:11). In her own voice Sarah expresses her joy and declares, "God hath made me to laugh, so that all that hear will laugh with me" (Genesis 21:6). Sarah knew that she had received a miracle in her old age because her condition "seemed to be insoluble" (Trible, 33). That's why Sarah laughed. She could not explain God's inversion process of making her fruitful in old age. We cannot explain how God works in our lives to bring about deliverance from seemingly insoluble situations that we cannot solve in our own strength. Bruggemann says, "Laughter is a biblical way of receiving a newness which cannot be explained.... Barrenness has now become ludicrous" (*Interpretation: A Bible Commentary for Teaching and Preaching*, 182).

John Bunyan says, "Mercy laughed in her sleep when she dreamed of Jesus." When you look on Jesus, you too, will know unspeakable joy and laugh with Sarah who was barren, but she held the "Promised Child" in her arms; the fruit of her womb in old age, the baby born of the Spirit. Sarah exclaims, "I have born him (Abraham) a son in his old age" (Genesis 17:17). Abraham named his son Isaac which means "he laughs" (Genesis 21:3). Laughter has two meanings. Phyllis Trible highlights them both and explains that Sarah's words "hold ambiguity because the Hebrew preposition that follows the verb 'laugh' carries both positive and negative connotations: laugh with or at" (Phyllis Trible, 43). In Genesis 21:6, this phrase could mean that we hear about "a woman giving birth in old age and laugh at her" (Trible, 43). On the other hand, laughter also means that all who hear and *rejoice* with her are "laughing with Sarah" (Trible, 43). Like Sarah, we cannot explain how God's inversion process can make a barren woman to be fruitful. Herman Gunkel connects the inversion of Israel's fortunes (Genesis 18:14) to laughter, restoration, and precious seed in Psalm 126:1-2, 6. Because the people were filled with happiness and restoration, laughter was like a dream come true.

Rebekah's Twenty Years of Waiting

My name is Rebekah, the wife of Isaac. I am the one that Abraham sent a servant to find for his son. Some people have said that I am not the usual Hebrew woman. Just to name a few of my many physical activities: when the servant and his camels came to our tent in Mesopotamia, I volunteered to bring buckets of water for all of them to drink. I ran back and forth to draw the water from the well and filled the jars for the servants to drink. Then I filled the trough for all of his camels. They were really thirsty after traveling miles over the dusty roads. I did all of this before I learned that the servant was on a mission to get a wife for his master's son (Genesis 24). The servant talked with my father for a while and I heard him say something that sounded like a prayer, and I ran to tell my mother what I heard and that the man had brought earrings and bracelets and put them on me. Then the man told my father about his mission to get a wife for his master's son. All the things that I had done for the servant and his camels, he told them to my father. He had taken notice of all my actions. And he was so humble and reverent that when he asked my father's permission for me to return with him to be a wife for his master's son, my father said, "The thing proceeded from the Lord, behold, Rebekah is before thee, take her and go and let her be thy master's son's wife" (Genesis 24:50-51). I agreed right away, but my parents and brother wanted to wait at least ten days, but the servant was anxious about getting back to his master. So I rode back with them on the camels and as soon as I saw a man in the field, somehow I knew that he must be the one the servant had told my family and me about. That was Isaac. Without thinking a second thought, I jumped down from the camel and ran to meet him. Isaac grabbed me up in his arms because he was glad to that the servant was successful in finding a bride for him. Isaac took me as his wife and he loved me (Genesis 24:67).

Isaac and I were married for many, many years and we did not have any children.

Then my husband prayed to God for me to conceive a baby. Finally, I knew that I was going to have a baby because of the constant movement in my womb. This continual movement made me perplexed and the struggling caused me to cry out to God and question Him. That's when God told me that I was going to have two babies. I had waited for over 20 years, and now I was going to have two babies! But there's more. These two babies would represent two nations; one would be red and hairy and the older one would serve the younger.

The Answer to Isaac's Prayer: Two Nations in Rebekah's Womb

Although Rebekah is loved by her husband, after twenty years of marriage, she is still childless, seemingly putting the continuation of the seed that God promised to Abraham in jeopardy. So, Isaac prayed for his wife to conceive (Genesis 25:21). Isaac finds his voice when he realizes they need God's help to overcome Rebekah's barren situation because it is through his seed that the covenant will be continued as God promised Abraham. God heard his prayer and Rebekah conceived. Isaac was a praying husband.

After Rebekah conceived then she learned that she was carrying twins and they struggled in her womb, the pain prompted her to go to God in prayer to seek an answer (Genesis 25:22). Rebekah finds her voice and petitioned God for an answer to her pain. And God told Rebekah, not her husband, "Two nations are in thy womb" (Genesis 25:23). He also revealed to Rebekah that the struggle was a prelude to what will happen after the babies are born and fully grown (Genesis 25:23). Rebekah is the only matriarch who received a divine oracle from God about the future of her unborn sons. Before the twins are born, God seems to be preparing Rebekah (not Isaac) for the future of her unborn sons. It was Rebekah, not her husband, who learns that the last child born (Jacob) would become the one to inherit the promise.

Just when you think you have it all figured out, God will surprise you in a reversal. The promise of the seed's continuation is often hidden in the strife, and the promise is also hidden in the reversal of the birth order. God responds to her petition and even gives her prophetic knowledge regarding the destiny of her unborn babies (Jacob and Esau) - the prophecy of two nations birthed through the twins (Genesis 25:22-23). The last in birth order, Jacob, would become the progenitor of the twelve tribes of Israel.

Beautiful, Barren and Favorite Wife

True beauty does not reside on the surface. It is an inward quality developed through a relationship with Jesus Christ, the son of the only true God. Rachel's barren wife motif represents a study in learning the difference between inward and outward beauty. Rachel's beautiful surface appearance was not a qualification of her fertility. Her fruitfulness was a result of God remembering and opening her closed womb. Rachel is the third generation of Abraham's family. She is Jacob's beautiful, favorite wife. Although her outward appearance was beautiful, she was also barren. But Leah, Jacob's first wife had many children, so to cover her shame, Rachel used a surrogate mother to produce children. "It is this barrenness that becomes the premise of all that follows – rivalry of sisters, the motivation for the device of the maids as surrogate mothers," claims Walter Brueggemann (*Interpretation: A Bible Commentary for Teaching and Preaching, 254*).

When Rachel bore Jacob no children, she became envious and said to Jacob, "Give me children or I shall die!" (Genesis 30:1). Rachel's plaintive cry focused on her pain, emptiness and heartache of barrenness. Jacob responded in anger, "Am I in the place of God, who has withheld from you the fruit of the womb?" (Genesis 30:2). Jacob's firm belief that he was not the one who had withheld children from her; God is the One who gives life. That's when Rachel decided to give her handmaid, Bilhah, to Jacob as a wife. Surrogacy in patriarchal times was an accepted Jewish practice (Genesis 16:2-3).

Later when Rachel conceived it was because God remembered her and opened her womb, and her barren condition was resolved (Genesis 30:22). She exclaimed, "God hath taken away my reproach" (Genesis 30:23). Rachel praised God for opening her womb, and she named her firstborn, Joseph which means "The Lord shall add to me another son." Sadly, she died in childbirth with the second child, Benjamin (Genesis 35:20). According to Brueggemann, "Both birth and barrenness, fertility and denial of fertility, are in the hands of God" (254).

Rachel's story is about God making her fruitful after waiting for her time. Timing is in God's hands. The Scriptures list other incidents where God remembered his covenant with Abraham (Exodus 2:24); God's holy promise to His servant, Abraham, who brought forth the people with joy and gladness (Psalm 105:42-43). After a time of waiting, God remembered Hannah and enabled her to conceive (I Samuel 1:19). God's remembering is demonstrated to His people no matter what their condition --barrenness or in perils. Nor does His timing of their being fruitful depend on a woman's age or beauty.

Barrenness is not a problem for human solution because new life is God's gift to humanity (Luke 1:48, 52). Because God remembers and hears her cry, Rachel conceived and gave birth to a baby boy, Joseph. Immediately after Joseph is born, Jacob begins plans to return to his homeland. When Rachel's barrenness ends, then Jacob's fruitfulness begins.

Jacob and Rachel's first son, Joseph whose name means, "God has added," was sold by his brothers to the Ishmaelites. Joseph ended up in Pharaoh's house and became prime minister of managing all that the Pharaoh owned. Later when there was a famine in the land, Joseph became the one who was the salvation of his family. New life comes in God's timing, not by human action.

Hannah Turned Barrenness into a Blessing

My name is Hannah and I am the wife of Elkanah, but he has another wife whose name is Penninah. She has many children and because I am childless, she keeps taunting me about my condition. Although I kept silent for years, I have been in misery. I don't blame my husband for not giving me children. I know that God must have a reason for my affliction. I finally decided to go to God in prayer and say all the things in my heart. I do believe that God is able to give me a child and when He does, I will give him back to the Lord for service all the days of his life. Our family made the usual trip to Shiloh for worship. But this time I opened my heart in prayer, I didn't want other women to hear me, and mouthed the words amidst the tears falling from my eyes that ran down my face. No one could hear me making my vow to the Lord, but I meant every word I said in my heart. I asked God for a son and promised Him that if He would give me a son, I would dedicate his life in service to God (I Samuel 1:11). Little did I know, the priest named Eli was watching me. He came over and scolded me for drinking strong drink, but I told him that I was a sorrowful woman and that I had prayed to God and I implored him not to think of me as a wanton woman. Then Eli blessed me and pronounced a benediction when he learned about my petition to God.

Brueggemann said, "A barren woman becomes a sign and metaphor of God's grace-filled reversal that is wondrously given in new life of Israel" (*Reverberations of Faith*, 90). Unlike both Sarah and Rachel who used surrogate mothers, Hannah never doubted her ability to be a mother. The writer of I Samuel does not describe her as barren; Scripture says, "Hannah had no children" (I Samuel 1:2). Hannah conceived and the Lord remembered her (I Samuel 1:19). Charles Spurgeon says, "A woman of sorrowful spirit received him from God, and joyfully exclaimed, "For this child I prayed." After Hannah weaned Samuel, she kept her promise and took him to the temple with her, along with a three-year old bull, an ephah of flour, and a skin of wine and dedicated him to God (I Samuel 1:24-28).

Tensions Between Divine and Human Initiatives

Hannah's song is the voice of a joyous woman rescued from the disgrace of her affliction which she told God about. In the New Testament, it becomes both Mary's song (Luke 1:46-55) and the church's song as the faithful community finds in Jesus the means through which God will turn and right the world (*Reverberations of Faith, 90*). Her story illustrates various tensions between divine and human initiatives. It is not just about a woman who prayed for a son. As Bruggemann notes, "The main theme is not Hannah's joy, but God's deliverance." Hannah's name means "grace."

Hannah understood the purpose of barrenness, unlike the foremothers before her. She neither blames her husband for her condition nor does she give him her maidservant to seek children to cover her shame and disgrace. Instead, Hannah recognized that her childlessness was given by God to accomplish some greater purpose. Barrenness brought Hannah to the end of her human strength to seek the One who could give her the life-giving Spirit that could produce the baby she longed for.

Although barrenness is the penultimate humiliation for a Hebrew wife; it is from travail of soul that God births Isaac, Jacob, Joseph, Samuel and Samson from closed wombs that He opened and made fruitful. The psalmist says, "He makes the barren woman to keep house, and to be a joyful mother of children" (Psalm 113:9).

God Still Answers Prayers and Opens Closed Wombs

While writing this book, I received an unsolicited testimony from a dear friend who told me her story of barrenness and answered prayer. Doctors told the young woman that her uterus was tilted and she would not be able to have children. She and her husband had been trying for more than a year, and she prayed, asked God for a child and believed God for an answer. He answered her petition. Her testimony sounds similar to Hannah's prayer and gift of children. This is her story as told to me:

> *We decided to begin a family after we had been married for one year. I went to the doctor after months had passed and no child. The doctor was nonchalant about it. He told me I had a tilted uterus and could not conceive or ever carry a child. That was the end of the appointment. He was very casual about the matter. Similar to Hannah's husband Elkanah, my husband was content with the fact that we were not able to have children, but I was not. I began to sit and pray in the room that would be our nursery; nothing special, just a very long conversation that would end with prayer and a promise.*
>
> *The view out of my window was so beautiful; it was a sight to behold. I would sit and stare at the mountain and just talk to God. I didn't beg*

Him anymore. And I never gave up on having a family. After praying and offering the unborn child back to God, I found out months later I was pregnant. I remembered my prayer and God remembered me. I have since told my children about the time I prayed for them before they were conceived. People always wondered why the second child was so close behind your first baby. My answer is, "I was afraid I would not have another child." At that time, I did not know the story of Samuel when I prayed. Years later, I was reminded of my prayer. Once again, I was back in that bedroom, sitting on the floor, talking to God. When I got up, I wiped away my tears, and moved on hoping that it was done. I wish my faith had been as strong as Hannah's.

I began to volunteer with child and family services so that I could be around children. We even thought of being foster parents. Then we decided to go to a fertility doctor. The doctor gave me a pregnancy test and I told him I had taken many and it is always negative. He told me it was his procedure. I told him of what the other doctor told me and I still had to take the pregnancy test. Shortly after the test, the nurse came in and told the doctor the result was positive. I sat their wondering what was positive. He said, "Well, I guess my work is done before I even begin." But I was still clueless as to what they were talking about. We were told not to tell family and friends until my fourth month because of my uterus. We went home in disbelief. I had no problems not telling anyone because I did not believe I was pregnant. It must have been some mistake I thought. I began to pray in January that if I could have just one child I would be satisfied and I would dedicate the baby back to God. I didn't know anything about Hannah's prayer. I wish I had known because it would have given me some comfort to know there is a season for everything.

As the months moved on, we told our family and friends. God waited for me to ask for what I wanted. I did a lot of crying and begging before, but when I got serious and asked for this child it took three months to receive the answer. I must have conceived a month after the prayer. I believe this was done so that God would get the glory and not the doctor who told me I would never be able to conceive and carry a child. It is no coincidence that when I decided to go to an infertility specialist, I found out I was already pregnant!

After that pregnancy, I rushed to have another child for fear I would not be able to have more. We wanted more children but two was all God gave us. I stopped looking for more and was thankful for the two He gave me. Several years later, out of the blue, we got pregnant again with another child. All we can say is, "Doctors may hold book knowledge but God holds the keys to all knowledge." What He says goes.

The devil did come against us during the last pregnancy. I had many health challenges that could have ended my life and or the lives of both the baby and me. But prayer works. The doctor tried to get me to have an abortion because the baby was going to have a lot of health problems. We decided that we wanted our baby and did not want to abort her life. Having a praying family got me through this time. And we still thank God for the healthy baby girl. To God be the glory!

Samson's Unnamed Mother

Manoah's wife is a paradigm and model of empowerment for every unnamed barren woman who believes that God has accepted their sacrifices and that He does not mean to destroy them through the barrenness experience. Rather, God is faithful. Manoah's wife was barren and scripture does not say that she nor Manoah prayed for a child, but an angel of the Lord appeared to her and announced that she would bear a son.

The angel gave her instructions that the child should not have strong drink, nor eat unclean food, and further states that no razor is to touch his head. According to a Nazarite custom found in the book of Numbers, chapter six, verses 2-8, this was a sort of prenatal care for Samson. A Nazarite is any Israelite man or woman who takes special vows of consecration to God according to rules in Numbers 6:1-6 and I Samuel 1:11 (*HarperCollins Study Bible,* 392).

When the angel appeared before Manoah's wife, she was reverent, silent, and obedient and filled with faith (*All of the Women of the Bible,* 325). Although Manoah petitioned the angel of God to return and then asked the angel, "teach us what we are to do concerning the boy who will be born" (Judges 13:8); the angel of the Lord only reappeared to the wife. The angel said to Manoah, "Let the woman heed all that I told her" (Judges 13:13). God clearly speaks to women and gives them instructions and trusts the woman to follow His directions.

In the context of other "Mothers of Israel", Manoah's wife appears in the recurring features of rivalry between wives and the dedication of a son given to the service of the Lord (*Reverberations of Faith,* 90). Because Manoah was unwilling to let the angel go and insisted he stay for a meal, the angel instructs him to offer the food as a burnt offering to God instead. When Manoah asked the man's name, his response was, "It is too extraordinary." Then the angel ascended in the flame offering; that's when Manoah knew that the stranger was sent by God and said, "We shall surely die, because we have seen God." But his wife believed, "If the Lord were pleased to kill us, He would not have received a burnt offering and meat offering at our hands, neither would He have showed us all these things, nor would He have told us such things as these" (Judges 13:22-23).

According to Charles Spurgeon, Manoah's wife demonstrated three extraordinary characteristics: (1) she had faith in God because she believed the angel of the Lord; (2) she was obedient to the voice of the angel who visited her and (3) she had great perception because she understood that if God had accepted their sacrifices, promised a birth of a son and made gracious revelations about the care of their son, then He did not mean to kill them. Manoah's wife had no doubts about God. Her faith was demonstrably stronger than her husband's (*Men and Women of the Old Testament*, 280). The only unnamed matriarch is a paradigm of empowerment for women.

Interview with a Christian Couple

While writing this book, I was introduced to another Christian couple who had been barren, but God opened the wife's womb and she conceived. They shared their testimony with me over several days via the telephone. The following testimony shows how God worked in their life. At the time of the interview, their baby was three weeks old. I interviewed them separately. First, I interviewed the husband because he wasn't sure that his wife was ready to talk about the experience. But to my surprise, the wife called me to ask if I would like to interview her; I requested that she explain the treatment she received.

She gave the following details: the experience with her doctors, seeking financial assistance to pay for IVF (in vitro fertilization), and also about her faith in God. The wife stated that her husband was fully supportive and involved all the way, but added that she believed her desire for a baby was stronger than his. I told her that Hannah's desire for a child was stronger than her husband's.

As a technique for gathering information, the telephone provided a closed space where we could only hear each other. I could not see the facial expressions nor view any body language – it was more like a confessional booth. But the interview captured their first response without having to read a questionnaire and think too much about what to say. They did not have prepared questions in advance of my call. After the interview, both of them had an opportunity to review their answers (individually) for accuracy. I offered my gratitude and deep appreciation for their openness and willingness to share a delicate subject about the wife's condition. And I assured them that they would remain anonymous.

Interview with the Husband

Question: How many years were you barren before you and your wife had a baby?

Answer: Six years.

Question: Which one of you discovered that they were barren?

Answer: My wife. Let me add that I was not really ready for a child that first year of marriage. But I believed that God would give us a baby when we were ready.

Question: Did you pray about your wife's barren condition?

Answer: Yes.

Question: Did your wife take fertility pills or treatment?

Answer: Yes. When God says, "Yes" you will be in the mindset of appreciation to be ready when God gives you a child. We had to work for this baby. We fought for him. And God allowed everything to settle and take place in God's own time. When God allowed us to have a child, it is going to be special for us. My mother died a few months ago and my wife's mother died a few years ago. Both of them were matriarchs in the family. We believe that God gave us a baby at a time that we needed healing in our lives.

Question: *What advice would you give to other infertile couples?*

Answer: *Don't give up. You have to really, really believe and have faith that in God's time you will have a baby. I believe that God had to do some things to prepare me mentally to have a child. Other people told us many times that we would have a child.*

Interview with the Wife

Question*: How many years were you barren before you had a baby?*

Answer*: We had tried to get pregnant the first year of marriage. After trying for a year and a half, I went to the doctor and discovered that I needed surgery for endometriosis and the doctor told me that it was highly unlikely that I would be able to have a baby without some help.*

I asked her to comment on endometriosis.

Question*: How did this affect your infertility?*

Please explain what the surgery was supposed to correct and tell what kind of IVF treatment you had for your infertility. Also, comment on your reason for seeking out and reading the Blogs? How did this help you?

Answer*: Endometriosis is a condition affecting only women, wherein the lining of the uterus grows outside the uterus in the pelvic cavity. During a monthly cycle, the rogue tissues respond to hormonal fluctuations, including bleeding. Because the shed blood has nowhere to go, it builds up in the form of adhesions and can cause the reproductive organs to stick to one another and other pelvic organs. Organ displacement can then cause infertility. Endometriosis is a staged disease, with stage one being the mildest case and stage four being the most severe. The disease can cause extreme pain, though the level of pain doesn't necessarily correlate to the stage; a woman with stage one disease can have severe pain though the disease is minimally present whereas the higher stages may not cause any pain.*

In my case, however, I had severe pain that would last 4-5 days a month. Doctors made me progress through ever increasing strengths of pain medications trying to find my level of pain relief. I went as high as prescription morphine (with no pain relief) before I decided that the monthly pain was no longer worth it in trying to conceive a child. It was a very difficult decision to stop trying to have a child.

For two years I did not think anything more of having biological children. Instead, focused on perhaps adopting children in the near future or living a child-free existence; however, it was during the time when adoption was on my mind that I discovered my company would pay for IVF. Knowing that IVF would require me to have monthly periods again, I first sought treatment for the endometriosis. If IVF didn't work, I did not want to be in pain every month as I had been in the past.

The surgery for endometriosis removed all foreign tissue from my pelvic cavity. Due to the severity of my case, five inches of my colon also had to be removed because rogue tissue penetrated through multiple layers of it. Additionally, half of my right ovary had to be removed because of adhesions. I spent three months healing from the surgery before we started actively trying to conceive. Under the supervision of a new gynecologist, we tried to conceive with minimal medical interventions. We did Clomid and Femara (infertility medication) as well as assessment testing to ensure that both of our reproductive systems were working. Given that I was thirty-five years old and had known issues, we only did this for six months before moving on to the reproductive endocrinologists (RE) to be assessed for IVF.

For me, IVF was a simple process. Unbeknownst to us, we ended up saving a lot of time and money with the RE because of the testing ordered by my previous gynecologist. At our first appointment with the RE, I received my treatment protocol (the exact medications and dosages to take and when). My drug protocol was aggressive and I gave myself every shot that was necessary over the course of eight weeks. I actually didn't find the shots that bothersome or inconvenient, and if the hormones had affected my personality or temperament in a negative way, my husband surely would have told me.

November 2010 was spent going through the initial treatment protocol to get pregnant and on the last day of the month, we found out that it worked. When I was about eight weeks pregnant, the RE's graduated me from their service and handed me over to an obstetrician for the remainder of my medical care.

I am generally a private person by nature, so I couldn't really say if there were other people in my life who had similar experiences as I had gone through. I turned to the internet to find other women in my situation. I don't usually comment on what I read; it has been comforting to just know that I am not alone with what I have been through. I just did general web searching, and clicking on other sites linked from one that I was reading. In this day and age, infertility is still not discussed as openly as breast cancer. No one is going around wearing a ribbon and pins that scream, "I can't have a baby." Turning to the internet, even with all its anonymity, helped me to cope and now come forward to help someone else who may be going through the same thing.

Question: *Did you talk to anyone else, for example, your minister or seek help from others?*

Answer*: No, I did not want to talk about it with anyone. We did pray about it; however, the doctor suggested IVF. After discovering that the company I work for covered IVF and the doctors could treat endometriosis, I changed doctors and began seeking a different gynecologist in Atlanta, Georgia. I had the surgery and treatment. Within one month after the treatment, we got pregnant.*

Question*: Did you pray about this or seek help from a minister before making your decision?*

Answer*: During this time we were searching for a new church home and several sermons we heard spoke to us. We found a new church and began paying our tithes and I believe that God put these services and people in our lives to help us in the midst of this.*

Question: *What advice would you give to couples who are experiencing barrenness?*

Answer*: Remain prayerful. Find out what your company offers in the health plan when you need financial assistance for IVF. Also, call your health provider and/or go online to get information about IVF. One way I learned about what other barren couples were experiencing is by reading their Blogs. A Blog provides a connection with others who are going through what you are experiencing and you can learn from them. I followed one Blog every time that it was updated over the past three years because I didn't know anyone else who was barren.*

At the conclusion of the interview, I had a closing prayer with the family for their new baby and thanked them for sharing their testimony. I also told them that one day their story would be a blessing to other women who have experienced infertility.

Reflection Questions:

1. Which one of the testimonies speaks to your spiritual journey? Explain why.
2. What have you discovered to be most important in your spiritual journey with the Lord?
3. If you are barren, what new information did you learn from the interview that will prompt a discussion with your spouse, doctor, minister?

NOTES

CHAPTER FIVE

The Problems Of Patriarchy

◇◇◇◇◇

In the book entitled *Women's Bible Commentary*, Susan Niditch's essay describes the patriarchal age. Niditch states that "The tales of Genesis portray specific marriage practices, customs of inheritance and the rights of the firstborn...(and) attitudes toward family and barren wives" (14). A general description of the lifestyles of Abraham, Isaac, and Jacob suggest that they were the chiefs of wealthy clans whose livelihood depended mostly on raising small livestock (*Reading the Old Testament,* 135). Abraham settled near Hebron; Isaac had connections to Beersheba and Jacob lived in the area of Shechem and Bethel. Jacob was the most settled of the three and Abraham seems to have led a semi-nomadic lifestyle. Both Isaac and Jacob marry wives from their relatives in Haran (*Reading the Old Testament,* 136).

The Patriarch Abram-Abraham

The patriarchal period begins with Abram, who journeys with his wife Sarai from his homeland in Haran to a land that God would show him (Genesis 12:5). According to the chart below, the patriarchal years span from Abram's birth to Joseph's death in Egypt (*Manners and Customs of the Bible,* 53-54).

Abram obeyed God's instructions to leave his kindred, his country (Ur of the Chaldees) and go to a land that He would show him. Thus began Abram's journeys which led him to encounter difficulty and fears shown in the story of his trek to Egypt (Genesis 12:10-20) and to Gerar (Genesis 20:1-18). As Abram traveled we start seeing his character flaws; they are most prominent when he becomes fearful or when he is confronted with any difficult situations. Specifically, he lies about his relationship to Sarai to save his own life and compromises the integrity of his marriage by saying that Sarai is his sister. Abram's lackluster character traits put Sarai in danger twice with kings who would have had sexual relations with her if God had not intervened and restored her to Abram as his wife. God had made a covenant to bless him with land and children (Genesis 15:2-18; 17:2-21), but Abram not only placed Sarai in dangerous situations, he also put himself in danger of losing his blessings several times. Although God had made a covenant with Abram, Sarai was still barren and she lacked the faith to believe that she could have a child because she was past childbearing years. So Sarai gave her handmaid, Hagar, to Abram to have a child. He listened to Sarai and that demonstrated his willingness to participate in the customs and culture of his time rather than wait on God to give them a child (Genesis 17:15-16). God told Abram that Sarai would have a son and that she would be the mother of nations. When Abram heard this, he couldn't believe it and "fell on his face and laughed" at the thought of a 100-year old man and a 90-year old woman having a child (Genesis 17:17).

The Testing of Abraham's Faith

When God told Abraham to take his only son Isaac and sacrifice him on Mount Moriah, it was one of the most critical problems he had to face in his life. Isaac was a young boy when God tested Abraham's faith. Abraham got up early the next morning and took Isaac, two of his servants, and wood; he saddled a donkey and they journeyed for three days before arriving at Mount Moriah. Abraham saw the place in a distance that God had told him to offer the sacrifice, so he told his servants to stay where they were because he and Isaac were going to worship and return to them (Genesis 22:1-5). Without saying a word, Abraham took the fire wood and laid it on Isaac, he took the fire in his hand and a knife and they traveled together (Genesis 22:6). But Isaac broke the silence when he spoke to his father and said, "Behold the fire and the wood: but where is the lamb for a burnt offering?" (Genesis 22:7). Abraham's only response was, "My son, God will provide himself a lamb for a burnt offering." (Genesis 22:8). Abraham proceeded to be obedient to God's instructions to offer his son as a burnt offering as he worked in silence making the preparations; he built an altar, laid the wood in order, bound his son and laid him on the altar on the wood (Genesis 22:9). When Abraham was about to take the knife to slay his son, then the angel of the Lord called Abraham and told him not to harm the boy. Abraham lifted up his eyes, looked behind him and saw the provision for the sacrifice, a ram that was caught in a bush; God had provided for the burnt offering (Genesis 22:11-13).

There is a lesson for us to learn in this story about listening to the silence of God. Whenever God is silent, He is still working on our behalf. Abraham's testing was an illustration of listening for God's voice when there is a prolonged silence. We, too, should wait and listen for God's voice when He is testing us. He will provide everything we need. According to *Strong's Concordance*, the word "listen" appears only in Isaiah 49:1. In her book *When God is Silent,* Barbara Brown Taylor tells us how God teaches us lessons when He is silent. Taylor explains what Abraham does and reminds us of God's directions to him. After God spoke to Abraham and told him to offer Isaac on Mount Moriah, there was a continued long silence. Henri Nouwen says that silence is a teacher, too. Silence teaches us to speak and when we speak it is a "word with power that comes out of the silence" (*The Way of the Heart,* 41).

Whenever God utters a sound, He creates futures, hopes and gives life. Notice that God does not speak another word to Abraham until He called him by name. Throughout the long wait for God's direction, Abraham was "listening" for the voice of God. Although the quietness was deafening, Abraham continued to carry out God's instructions (*When God is Silent,* 61-63). Throughout the silence, Abraham kept listening for God to speak to him, but God was testing his obedience to His Word. Abraham passed the test of trusting God!

The children of Israel also showed great faith when they plunged into the Red Sea and Abraham demonstrated that same kind of faith - they believed God would somehow save them (*Abraham & Family: New Insights into the Patriarchal Narratives,* 2000, 20). The silence of God requires us to listen for His voice before we act, while we are in the process of doing what He has called us to do. Through silence, God gets our attention, and then we are able to hear His directions and guidance for our lives. Whenever you are in darkness and cannot see how you are going to come out of your situation, "Be still and know that He is God". Listen to what the Holy Spirit has to say and believe in God's ability to bring you through danger and destruction, even when He is silent. God wants us to learn to trust in Him.

The salient feature of the patriarchs' problems was a desire to maintain control over their individual situations rather than allowing God to work things out for them, and it is our problem today. It was also a problem for the matriarchs.

The information below gives the name of each patriarch, along with his year of birth and death, according to the scriptures.

Patriarch Chart of Births and Deaths

Patriarchs	Birth	Died	Scripture
• **Abram**	2166B.C.E.	1991B.C.E.	Genesis 21:5; 25:7

He was 75 years old when he entered Canaan and 100 years old when Isaac was born.

• **Isaac**	2066B.C.E.	1886B.C.E.	Genesis 25:26

He was 60 years old when Jacob was born. Genesis 25:26

• **Jacob**	2006B.C.E.	1859B.C.E.	Genesis 41:46-47; 45:6

He was 130 years old when he entered Egypt; he lived there for 17 years.

• **Joseph**	1915B.C.E.	1805B.C.E.	Genesis 50:23

Joseph was 17 years old when his brothers sold him to the Midianites. The Midianites sold him to the Ishmaelites and they took him to Egypt. Joseph was 110 years old when he died. (Genesis 37:28; 50:22-26).

Line of Ancestors and Genealogies

The patriarchs' stories are told through their line of ancestors and the genealogies indicate that the matriarchs (Sarah, Rebekah and Rachel) participated in prominent and significant roles due to their barrenness before birthing a child. Albert Soggin offers this explanation, "In the ancient Near Eastern world and in the classical world, the genealogy appears as the most adequate instrument for explaining the origins of a people or a nuclear family" (*An Introduction to the History of Israel and Judah*, 95). Some commentaries choose to call these narratives "ancestral stories" since they refer to the genealogies, itineraries and divine oracle of both patriarchs and matriarchs. Ancestral stories consist of various versions of oral traditions that have many changes and told from one's memory and interest. These stories are knitted together and passed down from generation to generation (*Oxford Companion to the Bible*, 247).

Also, we know that genealogy is told from the pen of male writers. Just observe the writers' stories in the first book of the Hebrew Bible. Sarai is described as "barren" and she had no child (Genesis 11:30), but Abram did not have a child either; however, he is not called "barren". In fact, none of the patriarchs are described as barren. From a patriarchal perspective, Sarai is the one responsible for Abram's lack of children (*Childlessness and Woman to Woman Relationship,* 29). It was Sarai who took action and made a decision to cover the shame of her barren condition by giving her handmaid to Abram to have a child. Nevertheless, both of them were disobedient to God. Both of them invited trouble into the family by opening the door and participating in a human solution to a God problem, rather than seeking and waiting on God. Abram shifted the blame to Sarai and washed his hands of the matter and told Sarai that Hagar was her responsibility. Hagar discovered she was carrying Abram's child and became arrogant with Sarai. Sarai's ill treatment was the reason that Hagar left the home seeking solace in the wilderness because Abram gave Sarai permission for her to do to Hagar whatever she was pleased to do (Genesis 16:6-7).

One of the challenges the patriarchs faced was living according to God's laws for their daily lives while at the same time dwelling in the midst of ancient Near East laws of the *Hammurabi Code* that permitted customs that Sarai and Abraham practiced in their family.[1]

---

1   *The Ancient Near East*, Volume 1, James B. Pritchard (ed.), Princeton University Press: No. 146, 1958, 154.

Isaac's Story

Isaac's life stands mostly as a bridge between his father Abraham and his son Jacob (*Reading the Old Testament*, 144). Albert Soggin suggests that scriptural details of Isaac's life appear to have similar characteristics to those of Abraham, but on a smaller scale (93). Even Rebekah has a more prominent role in Isaac's family. Although Isaac is the one who prays for Rebekah because she is barren, she is the one who receives a word from God with the description of the two boys' features and the prophecy concerning their lives, saying "the elder shall serve the younger" (Genesis 25:23). After Esau and Jacob were born, their lives represented deceit and trickery in their adult years. Rebekah participated with Jacob in a scheme by helping him disguise himself in order to deceive his father into giving Esau's birthright to him; a blessing that should have been given to the firstborn son. Although Esau despised his birthright and was willing to give it up, it was Jacob who cunningly tricked him into selling it for a pot of stew.

Jacob's Story

Jacob received his father's blessing by deceit, but in later life, as the adage states, "What goes around comes around." Years later, when he thought he was marrying Rachel, his Uncle Laban tricked him into marrying the oldest daughter Leah on his marriage night. Jacob had promised to work seven years for Rachel. Then his Uncle Laban bargained with Jacob for seven more years of labor in order to marry Rachel, the one he really loved (Genesis 29:15-30). Jacob had obtained the blessing meant for the firstborn son, but he seemingly did not have control over his life after his marriage to two sisters. He was in love with Rachel, but after Laban tricked him into taking Leah first, he worked a total of 14 years for Rachel – the woman he loved. Then the problem of patriarchy goes into high gear when Jacob's two wives begin to compete with each other for children, using their handmaids and mandrakes. Leah, the first wife, is fruitful but Rachel, the favorite wife, is barren. Jealousy and envy caused Rachel to participate in surrogacy in order to have children. Just as Sarai did many decades ago, Rachel gave Bilhah, her handmaid, to Jacob to have children. After years of barrenness, God opened Rachel's womb and she finally conceived. She gave birth to a son for Jacob in his old age and she named him Joseph, which means "May God give increase" (Genesis 30:24).

Jacob and His Family Move On

Jacob heard Laban's sons complain that he had taken away what belonged to their father; he even noticed that Laban's disposition toward him had changed (Genesis 31:1). This presented another problem for Jacob, but God intervened this time and told Jacob to return to his father's homeland. Jacob packed up his two wives and everything he had acquired while working for Laban, including a herd of cattle, sheep, goats and other domestic animals. With all of his possessions and family in a caravan, Jacob fled from his uncle's place, but to his dismay he was pursued by Laban because he thought Jacob had stolen some items. In fact, Rachel had taken some articles from her father and hid them in her tent (Genesis 31:25-41). This time it is the wife who participated in trickery and deception (Genesis 31:19, 33-35) that caused more problems for Jacob. To resolve the differences, Laban and Jacob made a covenant with each other known in the Baptist denomination as the Mizpah which states, "The Lord watch between me and thee when we are absent one from another" (Genesis 31:49). I remember repeating this phrase every Wednesday night after prayer meetings before we dismissed. The message means, "If you do ill-treatment against me, though no one else is there to see it, remember that God is witness between you and me" (Genesis 31:50).

When it appears that Jacob's troubles were over, he hears that his brother Esau, whom he tricked out of his birthright, is looking for him. In Jacob's latter years, he became a wealthy man, but he had numerous problems that wealth could not solve. Wealth does not exempt us from life's problems.

When faced with the thought of facing Esau, Jacob was fearful and sent his messengers ahead with presents to appease his brother. However, Esau had become a wealthy man, too, and doesn't need nor accept the gifts. In fact, Esau sent word to Jacob that he was coming with four hundred men to meet him (Genesis 32:5-6). This occasion - their first meeting since the separation - caused Jacob to be afraid of meeting with his brother because he feared what Esau might do to him. So Jacob had a prayer meeting and he struggled all night with the angel of the Lord. During this nocturnal encounter with the angel, Jacob came face to face with his flaws and realized the problems he had caused by deceiving his father and brother. In this encounter and struggle through the night, God became real to Jacob.

Jacob refused to let go of the angel of the Lord until he received a blessing. Albert Soggin says, "Jacob's story is a theological reflection of how the unscrupulous young man manipulates everything skillfully to his own advantage and in the end becomes a pious patriarch" (Albert Soggin, 93). By God's grace, Jacob received a blessing that he doesn't deserve. In the morning, a changed man built an altar - for the first time - in the place where he met with and faced his fears. He named the place Bethel (which means House of God) because God appeared to him and changed his name from Jacob to Israel (Genesis 32:28).

On his return to Bethel, this time at God's direction, Jacob was told to go there and dwell in the land. This time Jacob built an altar and named the place, El-bethel because he remembered that God appeared to him when he fled from his brother Esau. God promised that a company of nations and kings would come from him and he would inherit the land that God gave to his grandfather Abraham and to his father Isaac (Genesis 35:7-12). This time, God changed his name and said, "Thy name shall not be called any more Jacob, but Israel shall be they name" (Genesis 35:10). God established His covenant with Jacob - a new start and a new name.

Joseph's Story

Joseph's story "illustrates the spiritual journey of a young man who is originally not very congenial, who matures through suffering and faith and becomes a pious patriarch" (Albert Soggin, 94). Joseph was Rachel's firstborn son, born after years of barrenness. Joseph was a dreamer. As a young man, he brought back a report to his father about his older brother's actions, and they hated him. Not only was Joseph hated for the dreams that he told about his sheaves standing upright and his brothers' sheaves standing around his in submission (Genesis 37:7), they hated him fiercely because he was their father's favorite son and Jacob made him a coat of many colors (Genesis 37:1-24). Because of the brothers' intense hatred for Joseph, when they saw him coming to look for them in Dothan, they conspired to kill him, but the older brother, Reuben persuaded them to let him live. Instead of slaying him, Judah convinced his brothers to sell him; so Joseph was sold to the Ishmaelites for twenty pieces of silver (Genesis 37:17-27).

Joseph ends up in Potiphar's house and he became a slave in Egypt, but that's just the beginning of his life there. Potiphar was a captain of the guard to the Pharaoh and Joseph, who had the gift of interpreting dreams, was promoted to a ruler in Pharaoh's court (Genesis 39:1-36; 41:37-57). His gift made room for him in the palace. Eventually, Joseph became the salvation for his family who were experiencing famine. During the famine, his brothers came to Egypt to purchase food. Joseph recognized them; but they didn't know who he was because he had grown older. Joseph had grown older and had matured spiritually over the years and he had forgiven his brothers for selling him. When they came to Egypt to buy food, he provided what they needed without cost. Joseph revealed his identity to his brothers when they returned to buy more food and brought back his younger brother, Benjamin whom he had required as a condition for them to return to purchase more food (Genesis 43:4-5). He said, "Because you sold me here; God sent me before you to preserve life" (Genesis 43:1-45; 28). Joseph - the one who was hated by his brothers - became their salvation during the famine in Egypt.

Reflection Questions:

1. Share a time in your life when you faced fear and shame. How did you face your problem?
2. Did you comprise, lie, cheat or tell the truth?
3. What character traits do you admire in other people?
4. How do you treat others who have been less than honest with you?
5. What is the most important lesson that you learned from this chapter?

NOTES

Hagar's Journeys

Hagar, Sarai's Egyptian handmaid, took her first journey when she fled to the wilderness following the harsh treatment from Sarai (Genesis 16:6). Because Sarai was barren, she gave her handmaid to Abram to have a child, but when Hagar discovered she was with child, she despised her mistress and became arrogant. This caused Sarai to treat her harshly, so Hagar ran away from the home. But an angel of the Lord found Hagar by a fountain of water and questioned her about where she came from and where she was going (Genesis16:8). The angel of the Lord told Hagar to return and submit herself to Sarai's hands (Genesis 16:9). Although God saw Hagar's affliction, He told her to return to her mistress, and submit to her. Before Hagar returned to Sarai, she received a blessing. God told her that she would have a son and to name him Ishmael (Genesis 16:11). God also told Hagar that He would multiply her seed (Genesis 16:10; 17:20). Hagar is the only woman in the Hebrew Bible to have a theophany with God. She called on the name of the Lord at the place (a fountain of water) where God heard and saw her affliction. She named the place, Beer-lahai-roi (Genesis 16:13).

Several years later, Hagar made a third journey when Sarah – now the mother of Isaac, the Promised Child - decided to send her and Ishmael away. Although the decision was troubling to Abraham because he did not want to send Ishmael away, God told him to listen to Sarah who told him to cast out Hagar and her son. This time Sarah's hardness of heart was against Ishmael (the older child) inheriting with her son, Isaac (Genesis 21:14). Abraham gave provisions to Hagar for her and Ishmael and sent them away; she left with her son and wandered in the wilderness (Genesis 21:14). Then Hagar heard the angel of God call her name and asked her, "What aileth thee, Hagar? Fear not; God heard the voice of your son"

(Genesis 21:17). God opened Hagar's eyes to see the provision, a spring of water He had provided in a desert (Genesis 21:19). While Hagar and her son dwelled in the wilderness, God was with them.

Hagar's journeys reveal that she left the place where she had received harsh treatment from her mistress, first when she was arrogant with her mistress; therefore, Sarah treated her harshly. But God told her to return and submit to her mistress (to authority). The second time Hagar left the home; again Sarah was the cause of her leaving, but this time Sarah did not want Hagar's son to receive any inheritance as Abraham's first son, so she cast her out. Hagar called on God when she was in a wilderness experience because of her afflictions. God heard her cry and provided water in a dry land for her and Ishmael.

While you are on your journey, whether it is your decision or someone else's decision, the situation is beyond your control. Look to God and He will provide for your needs.

CHAPTER SIX

The Principles Of Fruitfulness

◇◇◇◇◇

A Sermon

Subject: Barren for a Purpose: Fruitful in Your Season

Text: I Samuel 1:10-11; Isaiah 54:1-2; Jeremiah 33:3

And she was in bitterness of soul, and prayed unto the Lord, and wept sore. And she vowed a vow, and said, O Lord of hosts, if thou wilt indeed look on the affliction of thine handmaid, and remember me, and not forget thine handmaid, but wilt give unto thine handmaid a man child, then I will give him unto the Lord all the days of his life, and there shall no razor come upon his head (I Samuel 1:10-11).

The host of a radio talk show called "Tough Topics Tuesday" presents controversial subjects for discussion, both the good and bad. Usually, the topics that he introduces are not discussed in our churches; although Christians, as well as non-Christians, have experienced these issues. The theme of "barrenness in ministry" is a hot topic that I want to address in this sermon. Barrenness in ministry is that state when you have a deep desire to fulfill the purpose for which God called you, but you aren't getting the results you envisioned – doors remain closed, you have more rejection letters than you care to talk about.

Dr. Rita Twiggs preached about this theme of barrenness in ministry.[1] She talked about how each of us has that deep desire to fulfill the purpose God has called us to, but sometimes the opportunity to produce is not being experienced. But the truth is, we are all barren for a purpose and the good news is that you will become fruitful in your season.

Barrenness has both theological and physiological implications. This theme captured my attention because barrenness was so much a part of Abraham's family. You remember that Sarai, Abram's wife, his daughter-in-law, Rebekah and his granddaughter-in-law, Rachel were all barren. This is three generations of women who were barren for many years before giving birth. While that's unusual, the significant fact is that God had promised to give Abram and Sarai a son. The scripture says that Sarai was not only barren; she was beyond child bearing years. Imagine that! God made a promise to multiply Abraham's seed, but his wife is barren. As I began studying the barrenness phenomena, God began to show me some things about my own life in ministry regarding this theme of being barren and I could see a relationship.

Some Principles of Fruitfulness

If we are going to be fruitful in our season, there are some things we must learn. First, learn *to pray* and *listen* to God, even when He is silent.[2] Listen for directions to hear what the Lord will say. Moses said, "Stand still, and I will

---

1   Dr. Rita Twiggs preached at Metropolitan Baptist Church, Washington, DC for the annual Women's Day service, May 9, 2010.

2   Armin Gesswein says, "Prayer needs three organs of the body that are all located on the head. The ear hears His word to us, the tongue repeats what we've heard from Him back to Him, and the eye looks expectantly for the answer" *Everything by Prayer: Armin Gesswein's Keys to Spirit-Filled Living*, Fred Hartley, Christian Publications, Inc., Camp Hill, PA, 2003, 91.

hear what the Lord will command concerning you" (Numbers 9:8). The Psalms also give us guidance about what God wants us to do. God speaks to us through the Psalmist's writings. He says, "Be still and know that I am God" (Psalm 46:10a). God gives guidance through His written Word. Second, learn to *wait* on Him. I know that waiting is the hardest part.[3] While waiting, there are some lessons that God teaches; these lessons are not just for barren women, they are for women and men who are seeking His guidance. Remember Abram, Isaac, Jacob, Elkinah, and Manoah, the husbands of barren wives. Only Isaac prayed to God for his barren wife to be fruitful. Abram and Jacob had already fathered a child with another wife through surrogacy: Abram had fathered Ishmael, Jacob had fathered sons with his other wife, Leah and Elkinah had fathered a child with his other wife, Peninnah. Only Isaac and Manoah had no children. But Isaac is the only husband to intercede in prayer for his wife to conceive (Genesis 25:21).

Isaiah, the prophet talks about the theme of barrenness in Isaiah chapter 54, verses 1 and 2; it's the key theological aspect of the barren wife motif in scripture. It is the centerpiece of chapters 40-66 - which is the opening chapter of the final section of Isaiah known as Second Isaiah. These chapters have been attributed to a prophet of the Exile Period; the 200-year period passed when the Israelites lived in Babylon, their place of judgment. They were in a place of forgiveness and God proclaimed comfort, the nascent of a radical new era and reassurance that He gives power and strength to those who wait on Him.

The prophet gave key words "listen" and "hear" when he prophesized about the humiliation of Jesus:

---

3   Renita Weems talks about how she learned to wait, listen and "Surrender to the Silence" in her book, *Listening for God: A Minister's Journey Through Silence and Doubt*, Simon & Shuster, New York, NY, 1999, 33-37.

- How He would be despised and rejected by men.
- How He would be wounded for our transgressions and bruised for our iniquities.
- How He would be oppressed and numbered with the transgressors and bear the sins of many.

After naming the sufferings of Christ, the prophet abruptly changed the mood starting with chapter 54:1. It was as though he was in another time and place in history because he literally shouts the words: "*Sing! O barren, thou that didst not bear; break forth into singing, and cry aloud, thou that didst not travail with child: for more are the children of the desolate than the children of the married wife, saith the LORD.*"

A Musical Revolution Births a New Gospel Sound

When I think about this change in mood, it reminds me of the transition from traditional gospel music to contemporary gospel when the late Bishop Walter Hawkins began the contemporary genre. They sang "Oh Happy Day when Jesus washed my sins away." Later, Tramaine Hawkins sang, "Change." An abrupt change in mood starts with a hymn of praise and transitions to welcome in the dawn of the New Age. New rhythm of music birthed in the sixties brought forth a new sound in gospel singing. Baptist church choirs and gospel groups started using musical instruments like drums and guitars. It was a totally new season in church worship and praise. Worship choirs were formed all across the nation and named after states and cities. It was a musical revolution. The eighties' and nineties' gave us performers like Richard Smallwood and the Winans. In the twenty-first century, artists like Kirk Franklin and Tye Tribbett had a hip hop sound in their music for a younger congregation in a new season - all about birthing something God had put in them and being fruitful in their season - a new genre of music that never would have been accepted back when people were singing the old gospel songs, but it was fruitful in its due season.

Barren Foremothers who Birth Sons

After a time of waiting, the foremothers of Israel also birthed sons in their due season when God intervened and made them fruitful.

Sarai was barren (Genesis 11:30) and she tried surrogate motherhood by using her handmaid, Hagar to birth a child for her. But the surrogate mother got arrogant when she discovered she had conceived a child from Abram and Sarai couldn't. Sarai and Abram had to learn that they could not solve their barrenness with a human solution; they had to wait on God's timing.

Rebekah was barren, and her husband, Isaac, prayed for her to be fruitful (Genesis 25:21), but she also had to wait for her season because God was bringing forth twins, Esau and Jacob, two nations in her womb. When the pregnancy became too hard to bear and the twins struggled against each other in her womb, Rebekah questioned God, "Why must I be thus?" Even when we are getting what we truly desire, there are some struggles and difficulties that we must go through after the time of waiting for God to answer our prayer. But the gift is worth the wait.

Rachel was barren (Genesis 29:31). She blamed her husband for her barrenness and made wild demands because she envied her sister Leah, who was having babies and making the tribe of Israel. Rachel told Jacob, "Give me children or else I die." She tried the blame game, but that didn't' work. Rachel had to learn how to wait for her season to be fruitful. After the waiting, and years of rivalry with her sister, Rachel gave God praise and thanksgiving for opening her womb.

Sadly, Rachel died giving birth to her second son, Benjamin (Genesis 35:20).

A woman named Hannah was barren and she called on God to give her a man child. Hannah's husband loved her, but they didn't have any children until Hannah called on God and asked for a man-child. God answered her prayer; she is the only wife to seek God's help in making her fruitful.

Lessons We Learn from Hannah

There are many lessons you and I can learn from Hannah. We can learn how to get a prayer through to God. First, we must take our petition to God; second, seek His purpose and plan for our lives; third, surrender ourselves wholly to His will; then fourth, wait for our time, a due season. Just like a farmer who plants a seed, there is a time of waiting. There is seed time and harvest and each season is different.

Another lesson that Hannah teaches us is to visualize the answer before you receive it. She viewed herself as a mother. The view that you have of yourself and what you are praying for God to do is very important. You will only move toward your destiny when it becomes real in your mind. So become involved in your deliverance and be willing to participate with God as He gives you direction. Scripture tells us that Hannah actually foretells the birth of five additional children.[4]

---

4   "The formerly barren Hannah eventually had a total of six children." "The 'Seven' children in I Samuel 2:5 simply means many, but at the same time also represents the ideal", *Expositor's Bible Commentary - Abridged Edition: Old Testament*, Zondervan, Grand Rapids, Mich., 1994, 383.

Barrenness: A New Testament Phenomenon

Barrenness is not just an Old Testament phenomenon. In the New Testament, Elisabeth was barren (Luke 1:7). Elisabeth and her husband were both aged, but the Apostle Luke says that the angel of the Lord spoke to Mary and said: "And behold thy cousin Elisabeth she hath also conceived a son in her old age, who was called barren" (Luke 1:36). Notice the words, "She was called barren." Elisabeth had to wait many decades before she conceived. But God gave her a son, John the Baptist, who would become the forerunner of Jesus. God uses barrenness for His divine purpose. Every time we find a barren woman in scripture, we can know that God had a purpose for closing her womb. God destined her as a vessel to bring forth fruit for the Kingdom, a leader for God's own people. But these special children could only be birthed in the season God had chosen for them.

Foremothers gave birth to Isaac, the Promised Child; Jacob, who was the progenitor of the Twelve Tribes of Israel; Joseph, a leader to save his family from famine; Samuel, the first judge of Israel and Samson who delivers Israel from the Philistines.

Barrenness teaches us many lessons and God demonstrates repeatedly the fulfillment of the covenant promise of children, and what God, through the aid of the Holy Spirit, can do. He can quicken a barren body, open a closed womb and give a child with a purpose and a plan.

Waiting is a Season

In my season of waiting, it was during a barren time in my ministry. But God revealed to me that I have time in this barren period to research and write about a topic that has been in my spirit for over five or six years. I heard God speaking in my spirit that He had another purpose for me. Jeremiah 29:11 became my favorite scripture: "*For surely I know the plans I have for you, says the Lord, plans for your welfare and not for harm, to give you a future with hope.*" In the next verse, God says, "*Then shall ye call upon me, and ye shall go and pray unto me, and I will hearken unto you. And ye shall seek me, and find me, when ye shall search for me with all your heart.*" This word comes to Jeremiah in chapter 32 when the prophet was shut up in prison in the king of Judah's house. That's how I felt -- shut up in a place and unable to move anywhere that I applied for an assignment in ministry. Jeremiah prayed and said, "God you have made the heaven and the earth by your great power, there is nothing too hard for you to do." After this, God spoke to Jeremiah a second time and said, "Call unto me and I will answer and show you great and mighty things which you know not" (Jeremiah 33:3). These verses encouraged me to continue seeking God's will and to write about my barren experience. Eventually, God provided persons who gave me new hope and encouraged me in the work of telling my story.

When God is about to birth something new in you, just like when the baby is about to emerge from the womb, you need to cry aloud. First, the water breaks. And your crying helps to release the pain of suffering. Water and tears are the lubricants. As you give birth to new life, you experience a different kind of pain, you cry aloud in thanksgiving and grateful praise to God who brings you through the pain.

The scripture says, "More are the children of the desolate than the married wife." (Isaiah 54:1). Think about it. The *barren* wife was going to be more fruitful than one called "desolate." After reading and meditating on this scripture, God began to show me that through my barren condition, I would produce a book that would be read by many who needed to receive a word of encouragement from my testimony.

When I was in Howard University Divinity School, I wrote a paper on Galatians 4:26-29. The assignment, given by Professor Michael Willett Newheart, included drawing a pictorial representation of the scripture. I remember at that time I couldn't wrap my mind around how to depict Sarah's offspring because the paper was too small. That assignment made a deep impression on me and a vivid reminder of barren women in scripture that later gave birth - its imprint was in my spirit. Several years later I understood what God was showing me and the message He had placed in my spirit through that assignment. I had to go through a period of barrenness in my ministry to learn the meaning of the message. Although you are barren now, you will bear much more fruit through the ministry of the Holy Spirit working in you to give new birth to what God is providing through you.

What is a Revisioning Process?

Since you are going to bear more fruit – this is what you must do – enlarge the place of your tent. My perception was too small and my vision needed to be enlarged. What I needed was a revisioning in order to see Sarah's offspring from God's perspective. Revisioning is one of the methods an interim minister uses when a church is going through a transition. Revisioning helps the congregation to see a new direction and a new dimension of their ministry. Revisioning permits one to see not only what is near, but enables one to visualize the future by identifying and clarifying goals. Revisioning provides a broader dimension of where God is directing ministry in terms of spiritual gifts He has given to your congregation.

God used the heavens as an outdoor movie screen to display a multitude of stars which represented Abraham's descendants. This enabled Abraham to revision his present situation and shift from the present way of doing things to an expectancy mode. God showed Abraham that his vision was too small, he needed to "stretch forth the curtains of thine habitations" to see beyond the "right now" that conceals the future. God used His vast sky to sprinkle innumerable stars - Abraham's offspring - to open his mind to a broader vision.

God will reveal new dimensions of ministry He has already prepared us to handle. He has already opened the door; we need to boldly walk in the path He has placed before us. But God's will for us is done *through* the journey as we surrender our will to Him. People we encounter on our spiritual journey, like the professor who gave an assignment that stayed with me for years, make a big impact on our ministry. God will use others in inexplicable ways to bring us to the plan and purpose He has for our lives.

But more importantly, our simple obedience to His guiding Hand in seemingly small assignments that seem insignificant, God's will and His plan can transcend the boundary of any prison wall or obstacle that keeps us from the things He has prepared for us.

While writing this book, I discovered Dr. Howard Thurman's sermon on barrenness. Thurman describes a barren person as "undeveloped, and underdeveloped, undernourished and emaciated, stubby, and stunted" (23-24). Thurman says, "Like a tree planted beside a stream sending its roots down to the water. Its leaves are always green. It has no fear of scorching heat; it goes on bearing fruit when all around it is barren and it lives serene" (29).

If we want to be more fruitful, we must dedicate ourselves wholly to God's service. We are barren for a purpose - God has a purpose and a plan for our lives. He wants to make us fruitful just as He did for the barren Hebrew matriarchs.

Reflection Questions:

1. What are some principles of fruitfulness?
2. Who are the barren foremothers in Abraham's family? What is special about each of them? Give the names of the respective sons for each.
3. What is special about the matriarch named Hannah? Describe her character traits.
4. Who is the unnamed matriarch? What did she do differently from the other matriarchs?

NOTES

Esther's Journeys

Esther's first journey was to the palace at Shushan, with other young maidens following a decree from King Xerxes who was looking for a new wife because Queen Vashti, his first wife, was dethroned (Esther 1:11-22). Esther's parents were deceased and she was raised by her Uncle Mordecai who was one of the attendants at the King's gate (Esther 2:7). Esther's beauty brought her into the King's palace, but she did not let it be known that she was a Jew (Esther 2:10). When Esther was brought before the King, she won favor in his sight. Since King Xerxes loved her more than the other maidens, he put the royal crown upon her head and made her his new queen (Esther 2:15-17).

A Plot to Kill the Jews

Mordecai learned of a plot that one of the King's confidants had devised to destroy and kill all the Jews in one day. Mordecai charged Esther to go before the King and plead on behalf of her people (Esther 4:13-14). Esther sent word to her uncle to have her people fast for her before going before the King because she had not been summoned and could be put to death. Esther positioned herself to be Queen, but her uncle reminded her that if she held her peace and would not support the Jews, her life would not be spared any more than any other Jew.

Following a three-day fast, Queen Esther was prepared to risk her life to save the Jews; however, Esther had a three-part plan. She did not rush into the meeting with the King without preparation. After fasting, the first thing she did was to take off her fasting clothes and put on her royal regalia that symbolized royal rights. Then she entered the royal court of the King's palace to obtain his favor dressed in her royal robes. Esther waited for the King's permission to gain entrance. When he extended the golden scepter to her – which signaled the King's favor, then Queen Esther approached the throne and touched the top of the scepter which signaled her desire to be heard. As a Queen, Esther made her request in the form of a question, but as a gracious hostess, she extended an invitation to the King and Haman to join her in a banquet: "If it seems good unto the king, let the King and Haman come this day to the banquet I have prepared for him" (Esther 5:4). Queen Esther used protocol and extended kindness to the king and his servant Haman who had been promoted above the other servants.

Queen Esther Makes Her Plea for the Jews

As a Queen, Esther was positioned to speak on behalf of the Jews and her position carried responsibility, not for herself alone, but for those in need of an advocate. At the banquet, Queen Esther was able to reverse a decree of letters devised by Haman who wanted to destroy the Jews. Haman had made plans to build a gallows to hang Mordecai because he would not bow down to him (Esther 3:2), but Haman was hung on the very scaffold that he had constructed for Mordecai (Esther 7:10).

Queen Esther made two journeys: her first journey to the palace at Shushan was a response to King Xerxes, the Persian monarch who was looking for young maidens to be his queen and Esther was chosen. Her second journey (to the King's inner court of the palace) was at the request of her uncle to petition the King on behalf of the Jews. She demonstrated extraordinary courage for her second journey because she risked her life to go before the King on behalf of the Jews. The book of Esther does not mention God's name, but the footprints of God are left in the inner court of the King's palace – the steps of a brave, young maiden who took a courageous trip to save her people.

CHAPTER SEVEN

Infertility: The Provisions Of Help And Hope

◇◇◇◇◇

There is help and hope for infertile couples. This chapter is designed to promote conversation and discussion for couples seeking to address the current methods of increasing fertility or considering alternative solutions for conceiving a baby. The "Help Section" is an open discussion on the moral issue and prayerful guidance. There is hope for the childless couple who desires to have a baby and there is hope for the future of the child that will come into the family. Hope is truly possible wherever God is present. Therefore, this chapter presents both help and hope, along with information about ethical principles, and current Assisted Reproductive Technology (ART) options. However, this chapter is limited in scope; couples should seek spiritual guidance from their pastor. In addition to spiritual guidance, couples should also to seek professional medical advice regarding the use of ART options.

Understanding a Complex Condition

Scott Ashmon and Robert Weise offer a compelling argument on the theological issue that God is in control of infertility and that those who prayed in the scripture,

God intervened. Hannah prayed, Isaac prayed for his wife and both women conceived. Also, the unsolicited testimonies from twenty-first century women received God's intervention when they prayed. Only one barren woman reported that she used an assisted method to get pregnant.

This chapter provides some help and hope to married couples who are seeking education, treatment and guidance in their decision about whether or not to use ART, if they have not conceived a baby. Christian, married couples experiencing infertility also have concerns about the moral question about the various ART methods. In this chapter, I try to shed some light on the complex condition of infertility that affects many married couples. Much material has been published about this topic by the Centers for Disease Control (CDC) and nurse practitioners.

The CDC published a Fact Sheet dated July 1, 2009 that reported ten percent of women in the United States between the ages of 15-44 have difficulty getting pregnant or staying pregnant (2). A number of factors were listed as the cause of infertility and revealed that most causes of infertility in women are problems with ovulation. It is important to note that many things can change a woman's ability to become pregnant. The CDC listed nine areas: age, smoking, excess alcohol use, stress, poor diet, athletic training, overweight or underweight, sexually transmitted infections and health problems that cause hormonal changes (CDC, 5). Women are not alone in the struggle with infertility, men struggle as well - so it is not just a female problem.

There are several factors that cause infertility in men. Most often the causes are: (1) varicocele, this happens when the veins of a man's testicles are too large; (2) other factors cause a man to make too few sperm or none at all; (3) movement of the sperm, this may be caused by the shape of the sperm; and (4) sometimes problems start later in life due to illness or injury (CDC, 3). The Society of Assisted Reproduction

Technology also published a fact sheet with a breakdown of both male and female factors.

There is some good news. For couples who use infertility treatments, the report noted both success and some limitations. While only five percent of infertility cases are "unexplained", there are eighty-five to ninety cases that are treated with medication or surgery (*Salem Press Magill's Medical Guide*, 1). To diagnose the cause, specialists recommend seeking help after one year of unprotected sex. Females should seek help from someone in the field of obstetrics and gynecology known as endocrinology. Men should seek help from urologists who specialize in diagnosing and treating male infertility. Dr. Marcia Watson-Whitmyre states, "The biggest problem that infertile couples face is the emotional upheaval that comes with the diagnosis of the infertility and women feel that their self-worth is diminished" (*Salem Press Magills's Medical Guide*, 6). For Christian, married couples, there is also a need to have a discussion on the moral question involved with infertility treatments.

What about the Moral/Ethical Question?

Infertility and faith are concerns for the Christian, married couple. While all infertile couples suffer physically and emotionally, Ashmon and Weise recognize that Christian infertile couples suffer spiritually as well. Their arguments focus on scriptures that help couples meditate on God's will. God may be "directing them to remain childless and to understand the parameters of God's role in procreation, and to know that God may use barrenness to direct a married couple's Christian vocation or an opportunity for adoption" (*Give Me Children, or I Die*, 344). Compassionate support is an important aspect in the couple's decision whether to use ART.

As a result of the methods outlined in chapter three of this book, this section relates to the use of technology and the moral question. To use ART means "using technical means to assist the marital act's natural fruitfulness is morally acceptable, but doing so to satisfy desire for a prospective child as a means to parental fulfillment vitiates any use of technical means" (*Difficult Moral Questions*, 3). One of the models presented by Grisez and his colleagues gives hope for adoption as another alternative solution.

While couples desire to have a child from one's own flesh, it may not be possible and adoption presents an opportunity for them to open their hearts to receive a gift of life, a free gift from God. When a couple opens up their hearts and home to a child who truly needs caring parents, they can show the love of Christ and receive the blessing and joy of parenthood. Grisez and his colleagues emphasize that as we understand and learn that fertility is a gift of God, we also grow in our knowledge that we can be fulfilled for our desire for children in other ways, such as adoption or providing care for homeless children affected by traumatic family situations.

In *The Way of the Lord Jesus,* Dr. German Grisez and his colleagues ask, "May an infertile married couple try tubal ovum transfer with sperm?" While this discussion question concerns the use of ART, essentially a couple's decision regarding the moral and ethical question is having an understanding of these technical methods. But, some couples (like Rachel in the biblical story) become fixated on the goal of having a baby from their own flesh.

Couples may have different reasons for desiring a child. Sometimes the baby is desired for the wrong reasons, which means that a baby may not be willed for his or her own sake (*The Way of the Lord Jesus,* 7). With this knowledge of the various ART methods and the alternative of adoption, couples seeking advice on the use of ART should analyze their motives for having a child. Couples should prayerfully consider and weight the financial burden associated with any treatment, and seek God's answer whether they should adopt or use some form of ART as a means of conceiving.

Decision-making: Help for Christian Married Couples

One means of providing help and hope for married couples seeking alternative solutions for fulfilling their desire for a child is discussed by Grisez and his colleagues. They suggest that even when a couple's motivation to have a baby may seem sound, they question the following:

- Do you want to produce a baby by technology to satisfy the couple's desire? (2) Consider that the baby that is coming to be by means of in vitro fertilization (IVF) or tubal ovum transfer with sperm (TOTS) does not fulfill the couple's one-flesh unity.
- Will the couple decide to use technical assistance to assist the marital act by removing obstacles to fruitfulness? By assisting, the couple engages in a genuine marital act that remains the real cause of the child's conception.

This chapter presents a limited discussion; however, couples should seek guidance in prayer from their spiritual advisor and medical advice from specialists.

If adoption is the couple's decision, there is a different set of questions for adopting a baby. Adoption also means going through the decision-making process about the couple's motives. As Grisez and colleagues indicate, Christian, married couples who desire a child should examine their motives and critique them to ensure they are making the decision for the baby based on many things they consider for their self-fulfillment. A baby is a gift from God who will make their love fruitful and a baby will be loved for his or her own sake (*The Way of the Lord Jesus*, 12-13). Another resource to consult for an ethical discussion is *The Dictionary of New Christian Ethics & Pastoral Theology* (224). Both of these publications provide an analysis on the use of ART; however, the resources listed are not intended to be an exhaustive list of materials.

Reflection Questions:

1. What is your informed position on the use of ART?
2. Does your position have a scriptural reference? Which scripture describes your position?
3. Do you have questions or concerns regarding the use of ART methods that you need to discuss with your pastor or spiritual advisor? What are your next steps?

NOTES

Mary's Journeys

Mary, the mother of Jesus, made several journeys after the angel Gabriel visited her with the message that she had found favor with God and would conceive and bare a son (Luke 1: 28-35). She wanted to share the joy of her news with her cousin because the angel told her that Elizabeth had also conceived in her old age (Luke 1:36). Mary made her first journey to visit Elizabeth. When Elizabeth heard Mary's voice, the baby leaped in her womb giving Elizabeth confirmation that the baby Mary was carrying was the blessed child (Luke 1:39-45). Mary stayed with Elizabeth for about three months - they had much in common to talk about since both of them were experiencing a baby growing in their womb for the first time (Luke 1:56).

Mary and Joseph Journeyed Together

Several months later, Mary and her espoused husband Joseph, journeyed from Nazareth to Bethlehem for the Roman Emperor's taxation. By this time, Mary was about nine months pregnant. The baby Jesus was born while they were in Bethlehem (Luke 2:6-7).

Mary, Joseph and Jesus Journeyed to Jerusalem

Twelve years later, Mary and Joseph made another journey, along with their twelve-year old son Jesus, to the temple in Jerusalem for the feast of the Passover (Luke 2:41-42). On their return pilgrimage from Jerusalem, Jesus was missing. Mary and Joseph were worried about Him and looked everywhere among the caravan of their relatives and other travelers. When they found Jesus, He was in the temple asking the doctors questions. Mary was very upset and she confronted Him about their concern, but Jesus told them that He was about His Father's business (Luke 2: 46-49). Mary did not respond to Jesus' explanation. But she pondered this information in her heart. As a faithful disciple, Mary journeyed with Jesus from His birth to Calvary and she also followed Him to the foot of the cross where He was crucified (John 19:25-26).

CHAPTER EIGHT

The Postlude

◇◇◇◇◇

Voices of Faith

After years of barrenness, the fruitful wives' voices respond to birthing a son with assents of faith, wisdom and praise. In their own voices, these five women exhibit the principles of fruitfulness. Rachel had blamed her husband, but now says, "God has taken away my reproach and the Lord shall add to me another son." Rachel's voice is heard praising God for giving her a son and alleviating her disgrace of barrenness. While laughing, Sarah says, "God has made me to laugh, so that all that hear will laugh with me" (Genesis 30:23-24). When Rebekah questioned God, "Why," He responded by giving her a divine announcement. She is the only matriarch to receive an oracle from God regarding the future of her unborn babies. Hannah's voice is one of consistent faith in God - different from the voices of questions and protests - Hannah's hymn of praise echoes through the centuries. It was Mary's song of praise in the first century when she conceived a baby by the Holy Spirit (Luke 1:46-54). Manoah's wife had a voice of reason. She was an intelligent woman who explained God's goodness and mercy to her questioning and doubting husband.

Grace removed the stigma of disgrace through God's amazing grace and He gets the praise and the glory whenever women are blessed. I, too, join my voice in praise to God for the amazing people He sent to encourage, support and guide me on this journey. Since I have felt the distress of barrenness in ministry, I know that barrenness is a painful experience; therefore, this book is not only about the barren women in scripture, it is my testimony of how God intervened in my life to give me a fruitful ministry. But He had to teach me to see another phase of ministry that was different from what I had done in the past. Although it was a new phase for me, God used the spiritual gifts and the provisions that He had already given to me. Like Abraham, I had not seen the provisions until God revealed them to me. They were not caught in a bush behind me, but they had to be revealed to me. My perspective had to be changed about how God uses the gifts He has given to me for His purpose – that was a revisioning process. It was a rebirth of new life in His service.

Grace is the Answer to Barrenness

Since God's purpose and plan was to bring hope to the Nation of Israel, and Israel's hope is inexplicably tied to five barren matriarchs who are Israel's foremothers, these sons born in their due season became leaders in Israel's history. The sons' foremothers are women of strength and instruments of God's grace, which birthed sons according to His timing. Savina Teubal says, "These were not ordinary women, disgraced for being barren; they were very special women whose lives were closely connected to the service of a deity who cared for them and to whom, it seems, they had special access in times of need" *(Sarah, The Priestess,* 106). Dr. Cain Hope Felder, professor of New Testament at Howard University, School of Divinity says, "Some of these Old Testament women come to play a vital role as instruments of God in the history of salvation" (*Troubling*

Biblical Waters, 141). When He intervened, the barren wife not only gives new life for the family; there is new life for the Nation of Israel.

By grace the Promised Child was conceived by a ninety-year-old woman; by grace, Rebekah conceived twins, and two nations struggled in her womb; by grace, Rachel conceived and God gave her a son, Joseph, the redeemer of his family during a famine; by grace, Hannah conceived a son, Israel's first judge; and by grace, Manoah's wife conceived a son (Samson) who delivered Israel from the Philistines. Grace, God's amazing grace, is the restorative power that removes the stigma of disgrace from the matriarchs' lives and gives new life to their barren condition.

Theological and Spiritual Lessons

Barrenness is a subject that has both theological and spiritual aspects for instruction. Moreover, I believe that barrenness is tremendously difficult to understand. Theologically, the barren condition is a phenomenon for which only God knows the reason why He chooses to close some wombs. Spiritually, God teaches us lessons that draw us closer to Him to strengthen our faith, and to learn how to trust Him completely. Both men and women sought God for an answer to their barren condition to believe in His almighty power to give new life. I, too, sought God in prayer, fasting and meditation when my barren condition spanned five years of closed doors, symbolic of the women's closed wombs.

As a result, I have deep compassion and empathy for the grief and pain barren women feel because I have experienced similar distressful feelings in ministry. For me, barrenness was a feeling of not being fruitful, it was not a physical condition, but the condition was amplified whenever I received a rejection letter.

As I viewed my barren condition differently, I discovered God's direction for my ministry. He had closed the doors because He was preparing me for His purpose. This revelation did not happen overnight. Through the discipline of waiting and listening for God, I saw a different perspective of pastoral ministry. Not all pastors minister the same throughout their ministry; some serve in the parish as spiritual leaders, others hold administrative positions in organizations, and some pastors minister through writing and workshops, and others serve as professors and instruct in seminary and divinity schools.

Barrenness is God's own method of reminding us that we are to surrender ourselves as vessels for His plan and purpose (Jeremiah 29:11). Barrenness will bring us to the point of total dependence on His power for deliverance from our human condition. Then He intervenes and supernaturally opens the closed womb (closed doors) and gives new life in a way that brings glory to Him. It is like heaven's dew drops (Genesis 27:28).

This book has been a spiritual journey and the source of new life for me. I have received rich and abundant blessings, both spiritually and physically. Working on this book has brought new friends and acquaintances into my life and they refreshed my spirit. And God miraculously moved obstacles from my path and gave me divine provision through His miracle-working power. All praise and honor to Him who works wonders.

Reflection Questions:

1. What have you learned about your own spiritual journey since reading this book?
2. Have you experienced any barren times in your ministry?

Suggestions for Panel Discussion:

1. Have a panel discussion about the theological and spiritual lessons. Invite both male and female participants.
2. Invite a GYN doctor and/or spiritual counselor to give a presentation to your group.

NOTES

Saul's Youthful Journey

Saul, the son of Kish, and one of his father's servants was on a mission looking for his father's stray donkeys. Saul and the servant boy journeyed through the land of Benjamin, but still couldn't find the lost donkeys. Saul was ready to turn back, but the servant boy encouraged him to go on to the next town because he had heard that there is a man of God in that town and everything he says comes true (I Samuel 9:6).

Saul and the servant boy continued their journey together until they met some girls who told them that the prophet had come to town. As Saul and his servant entered the town, they saw Samuel coming toward them on his way up to the shrine. However, the young man did not know what God had told Samuel the day before, "Tomorrow about this time I will send thee a man out of the land of Benjamin...anoint him to be captain over my people Israel" (I Samuel 9:16). As soon as Samuel laid eyes on Saul, God said to him, "Behold the man whom I spake to thee of; this same shall reign over my people" (I Samuel 9:17).

Saul began his journey to look for lost donkeys, but in the process of searching for donkeys, God made provision for him to meet a prophet who told him where the donkeys where -they had been found (I Samuel 9:20). The man of God anointed Saul the first King of Israel and Samuel prophesized to Saul. Just as Samuel said, Saul met the prophets and God changed his heart. Those who knew him asked, "Is Saul also among the prophets" (I Samuel 10:11)? When God changes you, others can see the difference. God changed a youthful boy into a leader after Samuel anointed him.

There are times when we are looking for something else, something that was lost. While searching for the lost thing, God takes us on a journey to bring us to the One who will tell us what we need to know, how to get what was lost, and provide for all our needs.

THE JOURNEY STUDY GUIDE
For
Discussion Group or Partner Study

Instructions:

The author suggests using the questions below as a springboard to promote further understanding of the barrenness themes. Questions below are goals for learning. The objectives are twofold: (1) each participant will record their individual responses and (2) share in dialogue with another person or group of persons. Each participant should have a journal to record their answers. This same group could meet weekly or monthly to discuss a different topic over 6-7 weeks or 2-3 months. Close each study session with a circle prayer (members of the group form a circle; hold hands and take turns praying for each other; the group leader begins by praying for the person on the right).

1. What are the implications of waiting in order to produce fruit for the kingdom? The answer should relate to your spiritual journey.
2. Whether you are physically barren or feel barren in ministry, why is it important to spend time alone with God?
3. What are the steps for putting into practice the principles of fruitfulness?
4. What have you learned about waiting on God's promises?
5. Which one of the themes of barrenness speaks to your spiritual journey? Have you asked God to help you in this area? Write a short prayer.
6. What is your position on the use of ART? Does your position have a scriptural reference? Discuss any

questions you have about ART with your pastor or spiritual advisor.

7. How do you think the problem of patriarchy contributed to the barren wives' feelings of shame and suffering?

NOTES

SEARCHING THE SCRIPTURES AND RESPONDING TO THE HOLY SPIRIT: IN-DEPTH JOURNEY WORK

Monthly Devotional Guide for Individual Study

Instructions: Have a set time for devotions and keep your time with God. Prepare your study room with a Bible, a study Bible, pens, and a Journal. Use the scriptures below and follow the Devotional Guide: (1) Search, read and meditate. (2) Pray and listen to the Holy Spirit. (3) Write your journal entry and record the meaning of unfamiliar words. (4) Close each session with prayer of thanksgiving and praise.

Week One - The book of Psalms

Read and meditate on the scriptures in the book of Psalms. Spend time in prayer and listening to the Holy Spirit. Write in your journal what you believe God is saying to you through the following scriptures:
Psalm 10:9; 25:3, 5 and 21; 27:14; 37:7, 9 and 34; 39:7; 52:9; 104:4 and 124:14.

Week Two - The book of Proverbs

Read and study the scriptures below. Write about the waiting process. What messages do you receive in this book about waiting on God?
Proverbs 1:11; 18; 7:12; 12:6; 20:22; 23:28; 24:14; 23:28 and 24:15.

Week Three - The book of Isaiah

Read and meditate on the scriptures in the book of Isaiah. As you meditate on the Word of God, do you see a pattern in

these messages for those who wait on the Lord? Record the message in your Journal.
Isaiah 8:17; 30:18; 40:31; 49:23; 59:9; and 64:4.

Week Four - The Gospel Writers

Read the gospel writers' messages in Mark, Luke and John. For each scripture, describe:

(A) Who the writer is talking about; (B) what the person is waiting for; and (C) what is significant about their time of waiting?
John 5:3; Mark 15:43 and Luke 23:51

Week Five - The book of Job and the Prophets

Read and meditate on Job 1:1-22; 42:1-17; Jeremiah 14:22; Hosea 12:6; Habakkuk 2:3 and Zephaniah 3:8. Write a short devotional for each scripture using your own experience of waiting on God.

JOURNALING and DISCUSSION GROUPS
JOURNEY WORK
FOR

Small Discussion Groups
Or Partner Study

Instructions:

Small groups (5-10 persons) should select a group leader. The group leader will guide the discussion time by suggesting participants follow the four steps process below. Begin each study group or partner study with prayer for guidance. Form groups of 5-10 persons depending on the size of the group. Give persons adequate time for journaling, approximately 35-45 minutes. Limit each participant to 5-7 minutes for sharing until everyone has had an opportunity to speak.

This small group will last about 2 hours. Before beginning the study time, set the timeframe for each step. Review the four steps below. Give prompts as your group moves through your timeframe. The group leader will give gentle reminders about the time limit you have agreed upon. Make sure that each participant has ample time to share in the discussion group.

The four steps are:

1. **React** Write your brief reactions to each of the case studies, one or two sentences.
2. **Respond** -- Write your response to the Hebrew wives who used surrogate mothers to remove the stigma of barrenness, one paragraph or half page.
3. **Dialogue** - Select one of the wives and write a dialogue with her. It is important to be succinct and limit your

writing to one page. Share your thoughts about her actions; if you disagree with her, explain why.

4. **Share** - In small groups or with a partner, share your journal entries and discuss.

Ask participants for prayer requests and close with prayer for the group.

NOTES

Footnotes

Excerpts from Howard Thurman's Pen
regarding Man's Journey

1. Howard Thurman, *A Strange Freedom*, Beacon Press: Boston, Mass., 1998, 37.

Chapter Two – Pathway to the Journey

1. *The Original African Heritage Study Bible*, King James Version, James C. Winston Publishing Company: Nashville, Tenn., 1993.
2. Merrill F. Unger, *The New Unger's Bible Dictionary,* Database 2003 Wordsearch Corp., Moody Press: Chicago, Ill., 1988.

Chapter Three – Post Reviews of Journey Literature

1. Carol Meyers, "Everyday Life" in *Women's Bible Commentary*, 255. "The survival of individual households as well as the corporate territorial claims of ancient Israel was dependent on women for product labor and also for population growth. Large families clearly made the farming enterprise more viable, and an emphasis on having many children is characteristic of societies based on intensive agriculture."
2. R. Alter in *The Art of Biblical Narrative* (New York: Basic Books, 1981), 49, 85. J.G. Williams in *Women Recounted: Narrative Thinking and the God of Israel* (Sheffield: Almond Press, 1982), 48-55. A Brenner in *The Israelite Woman: Social Role and Literacy Type* in *Biblical Narrative* (Sheffield: *Journal for the Study of Old Testament Press*, 1985), 92-95.

3. http://elibrary.bigchalk.com: *Report on Infertility: Female Disease/Disorder*, Editors of Salem Press: Magill's Medical Guide, 4th Rev. Ed., 12-01-2008, 37.
4. http://elibrary.bigchalk.com/elibweb/elib/do/ document:set=search&groupid=1&request.; Marcia Watson-Whitmyre, *Infertility: Female, Disease/Disorder*, Salem Press: Magill's Medical Guide, 5th Rev. Ed., 12-01-2009.

Chapter Five – Problems of Patriarch

1. *The Ancient Near East*, Volume 1, James B. Pritchard (ed.), Princeton University Press: No. 146, 1958, 154.

Chapter Six – The Principles of Fruitfulness

1. *Rita Twiggs, Women's Day Sermon at Metropolitan* Baptist Church in Washington, DC, May 9, 2010.
2. Fred Hartley, *Everything by Prayer: Armin Gesswein's Keys to Spirit-Filled Living,* Christian Publications, Inc.: Camp Hill, PA, 2003, 91.
3. Renita Weems, *Listening For God: A Minister's Journey Through Silence and Doubt,* Simon & Schuster: New York, NY, 1999, 33-37.
4. *Expositor's Bible Commentary*, Abridged Edition: Old Testament, Zondervan: Grand Rapids, Mich., 1994, 383.

Bibliography

Alter, Robert. *The Art of Biblical Narrative,* Basic Books: New York, 1981.

Ashmon, Robert W. and Scott Weise, "Give Me Children, Or I Will Die: Procreation is God's Work." *Concordia Journal,* 24 (1998): 337-45.

Barker, Kenneth L. and John Kohlenberger III, (eds.), *The Expositor's Bible Commentary: Old Testament,* Zondervan: Grand Rapids, 1994.

_____. *The Expositor's Bible Commentary: New Testament,* Zondervan: Grand Rapids, 1994.

Baskin, Judith R., "Rabbinic Reflections on the Barren Wife." *Harvard Theological Review,* 82 (1989):101-4.

Boadt, Lawrence. *Reading the Old Testament: An Introduction,* Paulist Press: New York, NY, 1984.

Brenner, Athalya. "The Israelite Woman: Social Role and Literacy Type" in *Biblical Narrative,* Sheffield: *Journal for the Study of Old Testament Press,* 1985.

Brueggemann, Walter. *Reverberations of Faith: A Theological Handbook of Old Testament Themes,* Westminster John Knox Press: Louisville, Kentucky, 2002.

_____. *Old Testament Theology: Essays on Structure, Theme, and Text*, Augsburg Fortress: Minneapolis, MN, 1992.

_____. *Interpretation: A Bible Commentary of Teaching and Preaching*, John Knox Press: Atlanta, Georgia, 1982.

Callaway, Mary. "Sing, O Barren One: A Study in Comparative Midrash" *Society of Biblical Literature, Dissertation Series*, Scholars Press: Atlanta, Georgia, 1986, 59-72.

Cook, Joan. "Hannah's Desire, God's Design", *Journal for the Study of the Old Testament Supplement Series, 282*, Sheffield Academic Press: Sheffield, England, 1999, 10-21.

Damazio, Frank. *From Barrenness to Fruitfulness*, Regal Books: Ventura, Calif., 1998.

Deen, Edith. *All of The Women of The Bible*, Harper & Row: New York, NY, 1955.

Derck, Sarah. "Barrenness in the Old Testament: Recovering the Metaphor, A Thesis", *Nazarene Theological Seminary*: Kansas City, Missouri, 2002, 6-19, 91-95.

Dresner, Samuel H. "Barren Rachel." *Judaism,* 40, 1991: 442-51.

Felder, Cain Hope. *Troubling Biblical Waters: Race, Class and Family*, Orbis Books: Maryknoll, New York, 1997.

Frymer-Kensky, Tikva. "Rachel" in *Women in Scripture,* Carol Meyers, General Editor, Houghton Mifflin Company: Boston, Mass., 2000.

Graham, Billy. *The Journey: How to Live by Faith in an Uncertain World*, W Publishing Group: Nashville, Tenn., 2006.

Grisez, German & Colleagues, *The Way of the Lord Jesus*, Question 52: "May an infertile married couple try tubal ovum transfer with sperm?" Vol. 3, 1997, www.twotlj.org/G-3-52.

Hartley, Fred. *Everything by Prayer: Armin Gesswein's Keys to Spirit-Filled Living,* Christian Publications, Inc., Camp Hill, PA, 2003, 91.

Havrelock, Rachel. "The Myth of Birthing the Hero: Heroic Barrenness in the Hebrew Bible." *Biblical Interpretation,* 16, 2008, 154-178.

Johns, Claude Hermann Walter, L.W. King (translator); "Babylonian Law: Code of Hammurabi" in *Internet Ancient History Sourcebook,* www.gopher://gopher.vt.edu.

McKenzie, Vashi Murphy. *Swapping Housewives: Rachel and Jacob and Leah,* Pilgrim Press: Cleveland, Ohio, 2007.

Meyers, Carol. "Barren Woman" in *Women in Scripture,* Houghton Mifflin Company: Boston, Mass, 2000.

Newsom, Carol A. and Sharon H. Ringe (eds.) *Women's Bible Commentary,* Westminster John Knox Press: Louisville, KY, 1998.

Nouwen, Henri J.M. *The Way of the Heart,* Ballantine Books: New York, NY, 1981.

Powell, John. *The Challenge of Faith,* Thomas More: Allen, TX, 1998.

Pritchard, James. *The Ancient Near East: Volume 1 An Anthology of Texts and Pictures,* Princeton University Press: Princeton, NJ, No. 146, 1958.

Ruether, Rosemary Radford. "Woman as Oppressed, Woman as Liberated in the Scriptures" in *Spinning a Sacred Yarn*, Pilgrim Press: New York, NY, 1983, 181-186.

Shanks, Hershel (ed.), *Abraham & Family: New Insights Into the Patriarchal Narratives*, Biblical Archaeology Society: Washington, D.C., 2000, 20.

Smith, William. *Smith's Bible Commentary Dictionary*, F.M and M.A Pelouchet (revised and edited), Thomas Nelson Publishers: Nashville, TN, 1863.

Taylor, Barbara Brown. When God is Silent, Cowley Publications: Cambridge, Mass., 1998.

Teubal, Savina J. *Sarah The Priestess: The First Matriarch of Genesis*, Swallow Press: Athens, Ohio, 1984.

Thurman, Howard, Walter Earl Fluker and Catherine Tumber (eds.*), A Strange Freedom,* Beacon Press: Boston, Mass., 1998, 23-29, 37.

Trible, Phyllis and Letty M. Russell (eds.*), Hagar, Sarah, and Their Children: Jewish, Christian, and Muslim Perspectives*, Westminster John Knox Press: Louisville, KY, 2006.

Unger, Merrill. *The New Unger's Bible Dictionary*, Database 2003 Wordsearch Corp., Moody Press: Chicago, Ill., 1988.

Watson-Whitmyre. "Infertility: Female, Disease/Disorder", Salem PressMagills Medical Guide (5th Rev.), 2009.

_____. "Infertility: Female, Disease/Disorder", Medical Guide (4th Rev.), 12/01/2008, 37.

Weems, Renita J. *Listening for God: A Minister's Journey through Silence and Doubt.* Simon & Schuster: New York, NY, 1999.

_____. *Just a Sister Away,* Lura Media: San Diego, Calif., 1988, 1-19.

Williams, James G., "Women Recounted: Narrative Thinking and the God of Israel", Sheffield: Academic Press, 1982.

_____. "Beautiful and the Barren: Conventions in Biblical Type-Scenes" *Journal for the Study of the Old Testament,* 17, 1980, 107-19.

References

Conversations with God: Two Centuries of Prayers by African Americans. James Melvin Washington (ed.), "Afterword: A Scholar's Benediction", James Melvin Washington, Harper Collins: New York, 1994, 285-86.

Illustrated Manners and Customs of the Bible, J.I. Packer and M.C. Tenney, (eds.) Thomas Nelson Publishers: Nashville, 1980.

The Holy Bible, King James Version, Hendrickson Publishers, Inc.: Peabody, MA, 2006.

Harper Collins Study Bible, New Revised and Updated, HarperCollins Publishers: New York, NY, 2006.

http://www.biblestudy.org/question/barrwomn.html 10/10/2007

New Interpreter's Bible Twelve Volume Commentary, CD-ROM, Abingdon Press: Vol. 6, 2002.

New Seeds of Contemplation, Thomas Merton, New Directions Publishing Corporation: New York, NY, 1961.

Thomas Merton: Contemplative Critic, Henri J.M. Nouwen, Liguori/Triumph; Liguori, Missouri, 1991.

Reclaiming and Strengthening the Lost Legacy of Women in Ministry: The Significance of the Daughters of Ruach at Metropolitan Baptist Church in Washington, D.C. Doctoral Project, Blanche Clipper Hudson, Howard University: Washington, D.C., 2001.

Men and Women of the Old Testament, C.H. Spurgeon, Charles T. Cook (ed.), AMG Publishers: Chattanooga, Tenn., 1995.

Faith Seeking Understanding, Daniel L. Migliore, William B. Eerdmans Publishing Company: Grand Rapids, Mich., 1994.

Dictionary of New Christian Ethics & Pastoral Theology, David J. Atkinson and David H. Field (eds.), Intervarsity Press: Downers Grove, Ill, 1995.

Easton's Illustrated Bible Dictionary, Matthew George Easton: Database Wordsearch Corp., 2008.

Thompson Chain-Reference Bible, New International Version, Frank Charles Thompson (Compiled and Edited), B.B. Kirkbride Bible Company, Inc.: Indianapolis, Ind., 1990.

Index - A Guide for Infertile Couples

Terminology clarification of GIFT and a moral analysis of the procedure

Nicholas Tonti-Filippini, "Donum vitae' and Gamete Intra-Fallopian Tube Transfer," *Linacre Quarterly*, 57:2 (May 1990): 68-89.

Help for female factors

Speroff L. Glass RH, Kase NG, editors, *Clinical Gynecologic Endocrinology and Infertility*, 6th ed., Baltimore, MD.: Lippincott Williams & amp; Wilkins; 1999.

Help for male factors

Minnesota Men's Health Center at: http://www.mmhc-online.com/articles/male_infertility (September 10, 2001).

Help for aging and fertility in women

Aging and Fertility: A Guide for Patients, American Society of Reproductive Medicine, Birmingham, Alabama: 1996 at http://www.asrm.com (September 10, 2001).

Help: questions on ethics and faith

David. J. Atkinson and David H. Field (eds.), *The Dictionary of New Christian Ethics & Pastoral Theology*, Intervarsity Press: Downers Grove, Ill., 1995, 49, 223-224.

Grisez, German & Colleagues, *The Way of the Lord Jesus*, Vol. 3, Question 52: "May an infertile married couple try tubal ovum transfer with sperm?" at: www.twotlj.org/G-3-52

Information on Infertility Organizations

InterNational Council on Infertility Information Dissemination, Inc.: http://www.theafa.orgFertile Hope at http://www.fertilehope.org

Centers for Disease Control Division of Reproductive Health at http://www.cdc.gov/Reproductivehealth/DRH/index.

Recommended Reading for Adoption

"Blessed Are the Barren" written by a barren couple who adopted http://www.christianitytoday.com/ct/article_print.html?id=52127 (5/10/2011)

"(O God our Father and Creator of the Universe) we find it too inconvenient to wait on Thee. Grant us the desire to celebrate the sacrament of waiting. ... Bless those who pray to the One who is able to knead, shape, and bake us into wholesome and holistic spiritual bread that can become a sacrament worthy for our children to partake."

- James Melvin Washington,
Conversations with God

Prayers in the Old Testament
Matriarchs and Patriarchs

Prayers of the Matriarchs	Scriptures
Hannah's Petition	*I Samuel 1:10-11, 13*
Hannah's Prayer of Thanksgiving	*I Samuel 2:1-10*
Rachel's Petition	*Genesis 30:24*
Rebekah's Prayer	*Genesis 25:22*

Prayers of the Patriarchs	
Abraham's Prayer	*Genesis 20:17, 15:2-3, 5 and 8*
Isaac's Petition	*Genesis 25:21*
Jacob's Prayer	*Genesis 32:9-12, 24-29*